The Zombie Gnome Defense Guide

THE ZOMBIE GNOME
DEFENSE GUIDE

A Complete Reference
to Surviving the Tiniest Apocalypse

Shaenon K. Garrity and
Andrew Farago

Illustrated by

Bryan Heemskerk

RUNNING PRESS
PHILADELPHIA

Running Press
Hachette Book Group
1290 Avenue of the Americas, New York, NY 10104
www.runningpress.com
@Running_Press

Printed in China

First Edition: August 2018

Published by Running Press, an imprint of Perseus Books, LLC,
a subsidiary of Hachette Book Group, Inc. The Running Press name
and logo is a trademark of the Hachette Book Group.

The Hachette Speakers Bureau provides a wide range of authors for speaking
events. To find out more, go to www.hachettespeakersbureau.com or call
(866) 376-6591.

The publisher is not responsible for websites (or their content) that are not
owned by the publisher.

Print book cover and interior design by Josh McDonnell.

Library of Congress Control Number: 2017964322

ISBNs: 978-0-7624-9155-1 (flexibound), 978-0-7624-9154-4 (ebook),
978-0-7624-6618-4 (ebook), 978-0-7624-6619-1 (ebook)

LREX

10 9 8 7 6 5 4 3 2 1

PROLEGNOMENON

Welcome to the wonderful world of Zombie Garden Gnomes! Whether your interest in these creatures is for fun or profit, we can agree that you've made a terrible, terrible mistake.

Perhaps you picked up this book expecting a delightful guide to Garden Gnomes. Everyone loves regular "garden variety" Gnomes, right? They leave beautiful floral arrangements on your doorstep every morning, they sneak into your home at night to mend clothing and organize your spice rack, and if you're really, really lucky, you'll see one riding across your lawn on the back of a bunny rabbit or a gopher or some other small woodland creature. Drop this book and get yourself a one-way ticket to Bavaria if that's what you're after.

Perhaps you've decided that your garden is too boring and needs an element of high-stakes danger. Or you've seen that famous ad in the back of a vintage superhero comic book and are sure that you can raise Zombie Garden Gnomes in your spare time and earn a little extra spending money. Or maybe those neighbor kids have been cutting through your backyard too many times this week, and you've had just about enough of that.

If you're still just thinking about adding Zombie Garden Gnomes to your landscape, there may be some slight chance that you might listen to reason. Visit your local library today and find yourself a nice book about more pleasant pastimes, like checkers, or starting a fight club, or building your own nuclear reactor out of a decommissioned submarine. Something safe.

Now, if you're still reading this, we can assume that your lawn will soon be overrun with Zombie Garden Gnomes, either by choice or because you've got some really inconsiderate neighbors.

Read on for firsthand accounts of the earliest documented Zombie Garden Gnome attacks, detailed reports on their physiognomy, practical (and impractical) advice on care and maintenance of the little monsters, safety tips, and even some fashion advice, if that's your sort of thing.

Editor's note: Published here, for the first time, are the surviving journals of Herr Rainier Van Poort, the world's foremost authority on Zombie Gnomes. Much of the original source material has been damaged by the elements (and Zombie Gnomes), but I have done my best to provide an accurate transcript of these historic documents.

I used a similar method in transcribing the journals of horticulture student Barbara Wong, which were recovered from the wreckage of the infamous Monroeville Winter Flowerganza. Please note that much of the information reprinted here remains unconfirmed.

To provide readers with a sense of just how widespread the Zombie Gnome menace is, we have reprinted a number of relevant artifacts. The gardening column "Gilly's Green Thumb Gab" was widely syndicated in print and online before the spread of Zombie Gnomes made gardening into much more serious business. Collected here, for the first time, are all the clippings I could find of this once mildly popular feature.

~~Dear Diary~~
~~To Whom It May Concern~~
In the event of my untimely demise

It had been my hope to follow in the footsteps of my father, who, like his father, and his father's father, and his father's father's father's father (we don't talk about his father's father's father, the blighter!) had been a simple pretzel farmer here in the village of St. Olaf, but the events of the past three weeks have dashed those dreams like so much salt upon a pretzel. In the wake of this tragedy, I've shed many a salty tear, as salty as ——

[EDITOR'S NOTE: For the sake of brevity and clarity, we've excised the next forty pages of Herr Van Poort's journals, which focused almost exclusively on the manufacture and consumption of pretzels and pretzel products. Please consult any of the dozens of extensive pretzel histories written by the prolific Van Poort family if you wish to learn more about this admittedly fascinating subject.]

On that fateful Wednesday evening, I noticed that my fiancée had not returned from her evening constitutional, nor had my faithful dog, my faithful cows, or my faithful menagerie of small, flightless birds. I had just settled in for an evening meal of —

[EDITOR'S NOTE: We've redacted another six pages here, for obvious reasons.]

After several hours of searching, I spied the only other living inhabitants of St. Olaf, sheltered in the ruins of the town's lone gazebo. From a distance, I could make out a pair of nervous goats and our town's mayor, who seemed even more agitated than his livestock.

"No!" he yelled to me from across the field, frantically waving his arms.

"No, what?" I replied.

Suddenly, without warning, a swarm of red, pointed caps appeared, as if by magic, and a moment later, they were upon him.

I will carry the sound of his screams to my grave, and perhaps beyond.

He hadn't said "no" at all, I realized.

He'd said "Gnomes."

I can't ignore it any longer. My mentor, the great agricultural scientist Dr. Ava Griebel, has gone mad. I went to work for her in the hope of learning from one of the world's most brilliant horticultural minds. But she spends all her time watching the laboratory garden through binoculars, muttering to herself about "rotten little buggers," and laying tiny traps outside.

Today I stole a look at her lab notes and made photocopies of a few of the strangest pages. Here are her sketches of what I can only assume are the "little buggers," along with cryptic and disturbing notes. What can this mean?

The Male

Weight:
Varies, depending
on state of decay

Height:
Three rotten
apples high
(not including cap)

Gnashy
little teeth

Beard
(very nasty)

Clothing
once
brightly
colored

Horrible
little boots

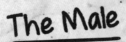

Odor reminiscent of spoiled porridge

Female

Braids full of bugs and such

Weight: Unfortunately not heavy enough to trip rat traps (must buy mousetraps instead)

Height: TWO rotten apples high plus one rotten strawberry

Surprisingly strong jaws

Horrible screeching noises when stabbed, also when set on fire (must investigate further)

Tattered remains of quaint European (Germanic?) dress

Arms come off with a good yank

Habitat

Attracted to gardens, possibly because
they provide low-growing cover and access
to unsuspecting humans. Mostly nomadic,
lurching wherever fresh meat can be
found, but will sometimes build quaint
shelters from the bones of the fallen.

Their interior decorating skills
are impeccable.

1. Eye-socket
windows w/
flower boxes
_____

2. Entrance
via jaw
_____

3. Sleeping/ digestin
quarters?
(must find out if
they sleep)
_____

4. Pet carrion
beetle?

GILLY'S GREEN THUMB GAB

HAPPY HORTICULTURALISTS AND HANDY HITS

of invasive carnivore ripping off an appendage. Readers, has this ever happened to you? If so, please write in with tips for Jason. And Jason, don't give up. Gardening may be slower with one hand, but it's no less rewarding.

Gilly

Dear Gilly,

With spring approaching, I promised myself I'd finally tackle that unsightly overgrown patch behind my shed. I went in with a trowel and gardening shears and was making good progress until—wouldn't you know it—something in the weeds bit my hand clean off. Fortunately, it wasn't my weeding hand, but the project is going a lot more slowly now. Any tips for one-handed gardeners? And is this my fault for waiting so long to clear the yard?

Jason

Dear Jason,

Absolutely not! Letting your garden lie fallow over the winter is an ecologically friendly way to let plants and insects hibernate. When you wait until spring to weed, you'll be rewarded with a healthier garden and a strong population of pollinators. I'm sorry that in this case you were also punished with some kind

Dear Gilly,

Your column on how to grow hardy seedlings indoors changed my life. Thanks to your advice, I had trays of peppers and tomatoes ready to plant immediately after the last frost. So far I haven't lost a single plant to slugs. On the downside, something in the garden ate my dog. Looking forward to the best vegetable crop in my amateur horticultural career!

Elena

Dear Elena,

So glad I could help! If you found that column (December, "Waste-Not Winters and Windowsill Wonders") useful, you might want to visit my website and browse the archives for "Sassy Seedlings and Sturdy Starters" as well as "Frosty Fails and Springtime Surprises." Sorry about your dog. Try Doc Bowser's Pet Care column for recommendations on pet cemeteries.

Gilly

Bah! Upon my arrival in Holland, my entire Zombie Garden Gnome Field Kit was confiscated by their misguided—yet perfectly charming, mind you—customs agents. It seems that my reputation as the world's foremost authority on and hunter of Zombie Garden Gnomes does not extend beyond my native Bavaria. (Or, to be more accurate, beyond the easternmost tip of my village. But I digress.)

Although I feel naked without my ankle-high flamethrower, whirligig-razor-blade shoes, barbed-wire shirt, and my anti-Gnome underpants, I hold no grudge against the airport security team, and in no way WISH THEY WOULD ALL GET EATEN BY A HJORDE OF RABID, HALF-STARVED ZOMBIE GARDEN GNOMES.

Fortunately, as the world's only foremost expert on the Red-Hatted Menace, I know all too well that improvisational skills can mean the difference between life and death. (Ask my cousin Hörst, Bavaria's only foremost prop comic about this, and he'll concur. What a country!) Armed with only my wits and a traveler's check that I had safely hidden in my non–anti-Gnome underpants, I made my way to the local garden supply store, the ominously named Gnome Depot.

Sadly, my arrival coincided with the start of tulip season, and the selection of bladed garden tools had been thoroughly picked over, as had the selection of blunt objects, and the selection of pointy, stabby things. I went to the manager's office to lodge a complaint, only to find that he and the cashiers had been picked over, too, as I found myself in the midst of a ZOMBIE GARDEN GNOME FEEDING FRENZY.

[EDITOR'S NOTE: Here the manuscript ends abruptly in several torn-off pages. The next entry appears to be a rough draft of a letter to a nearby pancake house complaining that what was advertised as a lingonberry waffle topping was in fact marionberry and also criticizing the cleanliness of the men's room. This passage has been excised, as its relevance to Zombie Gnomes remains unclear.]

Keep your wits about you and remember this helpful advice when you find yourself in a life or death Gnome battle. If you can spell the word "Gnome," this simple list will see you through any battle:

GAZE UP ON YOUR SURROUNDINGS.
DO YOU SEE GNOMES? I HOPE YOU DO NOT.

NOT BEING EATEN BY GNOMES—THAT IS YOUR GOAL.

OUTSIDE OF A GNOME'S BELLY—THAT IS WHERE YOU SHOULD ALWAYS BE.

ME? INSIDE A GNOME'S BELLY? THAT IS NOT A PLACE THAT I SHOULD BE.

ESPECIALLY BAD TO BE EATEN BY A GNOME IT IS—THAT'S WHAT I SAY.

AM I LOSING MY MIND? Today I saw one of the creatures Dr. Griebel keeps muttering about. It looked exactly like this sketch from her notes, but a little greener. Also, nothing in the notes prepared me for how bad these things smell. Like a gallon jar of pickles left in the back of a car all summer.

Though usually mindless and shambling, they sometimes display almost intelligent behavior. This specimen has made trophies of its kills and wears them with what might be called pride.

Chipmunk-tail cap

Human kneecap cape

Necklace of teeth (mixed, mostly human)

Shinbone staff

Songbird beaks, strung on mouse-tail belt

Toe boots

NOTES:

This unusually clever specimen has developed a method
of air travel. If more of them are capable of learning this
trick, I fear they could spread even faster.

   It's becoming harder to trap specimens for study.
Perhaps they're growing tired of the lab mice I leave in the
traps. Must find more tempting bait.

IN OTHER NEWS, DR. GRIEBEL HAS HIRED A NEW
INTERN. HIS NAME IS DAVE. SHE KEEPS HANGING
SAUSAGES AROUND HIS NECK AND MAKING HIM
STAND IN THE GARDEN.

   BETTER GO. I HEAR DAVE FIGHTING WITH
SOMETHING IN THE KALE PATCH AND DR. GRIEBEL
CALLING ME TO GET THE CAMERA.

GILLY'S GREEN THUMB GAB

Nosy Neighbors and Irritating Infections

Dear Gilly,

My neighborhood housing association has strict rules about landscaping. We're not permitted to grow vegetables, plant flowers in non-coordinating colors, or trim our trees freehand (diagrams and large protractors are provided by the neighborhood board). Above all, tacky lawn decorations are prohibited. I was recently fined because the neighbors reported seeing unapproved lawn ornaments in my yard. The thing is, I dont own any lawn ornaments. Any idea what the problem could be?

Chloe

Dear Chloe,

Yes. The problem is that you moved into a neighborhood full of Snooping Susies. Overbearing housing associations are something of a bee in my personal bonnet. Longtime fans may recall with particular horror the sad stories of Ted, who had to uproot tomatoes his neighbors judged to have "tie-dye" colors ("Prying Eyes

and Trippy Trellises") and Judy, whose promising career as a topiary artist was nipped, no pun intended, in the bud ("Great Green Gorillas and Leafy Lemurs").

As for the lawn ornaments your neighbors claimed to see, either they ate some of Ted's psychedelic tomatoes and were—in the counterculture parlance—"wigging out," or they're making up stories to get you in trouble. The best way to fight them is to run for the neighborhood board yourself and reform your rotten borough. Be the change you want to see in your garden.

Gilly

Dear Gilly,

Last month I wrote to you about the little hand-loss problem I experienced while weeding. The good news is, I finally cleared that overgrown patch, tilled it with well-fertilized soil, and planted rhododendrons. The bad news is a little more complicated. The necrotic patch around the stump (did I mention it turned gray and spongy?)

has been spreading, and now both arms and part of my torso are infected. Meanwhile, I've developed a craving for living flesh and I seem to have grown a long white beard. Any advice? I'd write more, but it's getting hard to type.

Jason

P.S. I want to eat your head.

Dear Jason,

This is deeply troubling. Rhododendrons should be fertilized sparingly.

Gilly

Very successful outing in Reykjavik last week, wiping out at least three hjordes of Zombie Gnomes. With the northern populations in check, I feel that I must now turn my attention to the Americas. My cousin Hörst (not to be confused with my horse, Cousin) has informed me of strange happenings in New York's Central Park and Boston Common, and I must confess that wanderlust has gotten the best of me. My destiny lies over the sea.

Perhaps there I may find the elusive secret to finally destroying the Zombie Gnomes once and for all.

And also "tater tots." I am not sure what they are, but I'm confident that I will find them in America.

***

The passage to America is long and arduous. I find myself tossed helplessly upon the waves, buffeted and battered as the hours stretch into days. Also, there is a charge for movies and the eastward route has all the ones I wanted to see.

I shall endeavor to pass the time by filling this journal with advice to the aspiring Zombie Gnome hunter. Perhaps my hard-won knowledge may aid others in the eternal battle against the Red-Hatted Menace.

THE FOLLOWING SECTION HAS BEEN BADLY TRANSCRIBED BY MY COUSIN HÖRST, SO PLEASE EXCUSE HIS YOUTHFUL ENTHUSIASM.

SO YOUR YARD IS HOPELESSLY INFESTED WITH ZOMBIE GNOMES:

A Helpful Guide to
Never Leaving Your House Ever Again

It's happened to all of us, hasn't it? You wake up after a good night's sleep to the sound of Zombie Gnomes scurrying around your front lawn and devouring everything in sight, and you realize you're (once again) completely unprepared for this miniature infestation.

Sure, you can call your cousin (again) and ask him to stop by with a flamethrower and an extra pair of high-top sneakers, but you know he's going to be a total jerk about it at the next big family gathering, or, worse yet, he's tired of bailing you out and he's not even going to answer the phone when he sees your number (caller ID—much like a feral Zombie Gnome—is NOT your friend).

Since a Zombie Gnome infestation can occur at any moment, you should be prepared to find yourself quarantined at any time, at any place. Here are a few tips to help you weather the inevitable apocalypse:

*Always have at least six microwavable pizzas in your freezer, in various flavors. If you're unable to leave your home, it's unlikely that the pizza delivery guy can make it across your lawn before Zombie Gnomes devour him (and your extra-large anchovy and pineapple special with extra cheese).

*The longest Zombie Gnome standoff on record lasted seventeen years, three months, and four days. But don't worry! On average, you can expect to be eaten within three days of their arrival.

*Make sure to have plenty of board games and candles on hand. You may have to pass many, many hours without electricity, and you don't want to call it quits on an intense game of Scrabble just because the sun's gone down and your roommate claims he doesn't want to play anymore. And you know he's only saying that because he's TOTALLY GETTING HIS BUTT KICKED BY YOU. NOT COOL, CARL! NOT COOL AT ALL!

*Oh, right, and you may go a bit stir-crazy after you've been stuck inside for a few days.

BUT THAT DOESN'T MEAN YOU GET TO CHEAT AT SCRABBLE, CARL! "BIGGISHLY" ISN'T A WORD AND YOU KNOW IT!

*The Zombie Gnome invasion is a great excuse to tackle all kinds of projects that you've never gotten around to doing. Organize your family photos! Write a letter to your grandmother—by hand! Fix that squeaky cabinet in the kitchen! And that $43 billion in stolen jewels you've been hiding in a secret location? Time to finally get around to drawing up a treasure map and a series of clues to reveal their true location, just in case you get eaten before you're able to retrieve them.

*Keep about five times as much pet food around as you think you'll need, even if you don't have pets. Trust me on this.

*While you may tell yourself that you'll finally get around to reading classic literature like *War and Peace* or the complete works of William Shakespeare if the apocalypse really comes to pass, we know that's just not true. If you don't already have at least three shelves dedicated to romance novels in your home, you need to remedy that immediately. At least five books should have pirates on the cover.

*Did you know that honey never spoils? Either get yourself about three barrels full of honey that you can store in a cool, dry place, or fill one room of your house entirely with bees. Trust us.

*The play *Our Town* by Thornton Wilder requires very minimal sets and props, and staging a production of this beloved classic is just the thing to buoy everyone's spirits around the time your third week of quarantine starts. If you happen to be locked up with veteran stage actor Hal Holbrook, you shouldn't just assume that he'll want to perform his award-winning one-man play about the life and times of Mark Twain, but he'll be offended if you don't at least drop a few hints.

*To conserve energy, reduce the temperature of your indoor heated pool to a brisk 81 degrees as opposed to the more standard 85 degrees. It's going to be difficult, sure, but no one said the end of the world would be easy.

*Over 85 percent of Americans do not have an adequate emergency kit at home. Since you're probably one of those people, ask around and find out which of your neighbors is part of that super-prepared 15 percent so that you can borrow stuff from them when the Zombie Gnomes invade.

*Crafts are an excellent way to pass the time during a Zombie Gnome invasion. Even more important than an emergency kit is a well-stocked art supply kit. We recommend seven paper plates, six pounds of cotton balls, a selection of eight basic markers, and twenty pipe cleaners per every three people locked in at your house.

*Remember the "5-2-1 rule" when sequestered from the rest of the world. Make sure you get five hours of sleep every night, eat at least two full meals per day, and don't lose more than one important body part during each Zombie Gnome attack. You may be able to stretch this and get by on one great big meal per day, but if you want to survive, we must insist that you keep close track of all your body parts.

*When all else fails, your friends and family will always be there for you. If your back's against the wall, you know you can count on them. When the chips are down, pull them aside, tell them how much they mean to you, then drench the slowest of them in honey, toss them on the lawn, and run as fast as you can to the next town over.

Dr. Griebel is happy with Dave, the new intern. "You're such a good sport about letting me hang raw meat and blood-soaked rags around your neck, Dave," she says, loudly enough for me to hear. "Unlike *SOME* people."

With Dr. Griebel busy painting bull's-eyes on the ground for Dave to stand on, I had an afternoon off for the first time in weeks. I went to the campus library, planning to catch up on my thesis project (something about soybeans? I can barely remember), but somehow I found myself on a research database looking up the keywords "zombie" and "gnome."

Most of the results were incoherent "papers" and raving, threatening letters to scientific journals by some obvious crank named Van Poort. But I did find this odd transcript from an old White House press conference:

Director Cooper: And that concludes today's—
New York Ledger: Mr. Cooper! Mr. Cooper!
Cooper: Yes?
New York Ledger: Does the President have any comment on the disappearance of North Haverbrook?
Cooper: What disappearance in North Haverbrook?
New York Ledger: No, the disappearance of North Haverbrook. The entire city is gone, except for some scraps of cloth and some tiny footprints.
Cooper: I can assure you that the President had nothing to do with this. To even suggest that—
New York Ledger: I didn't suggest anything. I was just—

Cooper: To even imply that the President has unleashed a [inaudible] of Zombie Gnomes upon his political enemies is preposterous. I mean, how would he even control them? It's not like he's even got a team of military experts working on that, right?
New York Ledger: Sir, you're the one who—
Cooper: Heh. "Zombie Gnomes," indeed. Ha-ha. Next you're going to say their little red hats are popping up right behind me as we speak. Oh my God, they aren't, are they?

New York Ledger: Um...
Cooper: Shut up! You're the Zombie Gnome! THIS PRESS CONFERENCE IS OVER! TURN THAT CAMERA OFF! I SAID TURN THAT—

[Audible breaking of glass. Transcript ends.]

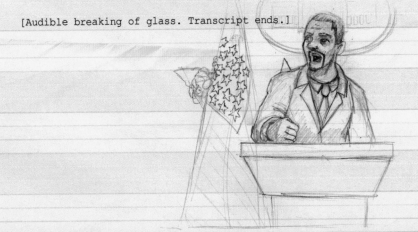

Searching for some kind of follow-up information, I came across a recently declassified federal government document from the same period.

Actually, it's still pretty classified, but it's all I could find.

I should probably go check on Dave.

August ▮▮ 19▮▮

The ▮▮▮▮▮▮▮▮▮▮▮▮▮▮▮▮▮▮▮▮▮▮▮▮▮▮▮▮▮▮▮▮
▮▮▮▮▮▮▮▮▮▮▮▮▮▮▮▮▮▮▮▮▮▮▮▮▮▮▮▮▮▮▮▮▮▮
▮▮▮▮▮▮▮▮▮▮▮▮▮▮▮▮▮▮▮▮▮ Gnome ▮▮▮▮
▮▮▮▮▮ tangerine ▮▮▮▮▮▮▮▮▮▮▮▮▮▮▮▮
▮▮▮▮▮▮▮▮▮▮▮▮▮▮▮▮▮▮▮▮▮▮▮▮▮▮▮▮▮▮▮▮▮▮
▮▮▮▮▮▮▮▮▮▮▮▮▮▮▮▮▮▮▮▮▮▮▮▮▮▮▮▮▮▮▮▮▮▮
▮▮▮▮▮▮▮▮▮▮▮▮▮▮▮▮▮▮▮ on top of the ▮▮▮▮
▮▮▮▮ awful little hats ▮▮▮▮▮▮▮▮▮▮▮▮▮▮
▮▮▮▮▮▮▮ until ▮▮▮▮▮▮▮▮▮▮▮▮▮

▮▮▮▮▮▮▮▮▮▮▮▮▮▮▮▮▮▮▮▮▮▮▮▮▮▮▮▮▮▮▮▮▮▮
▮▮▮▮▮▮▮▮▮▮▮▮▮▮▮▮▮▮▮▮▮▮▮▮▮▮▮▮▮▮▮▮▮▮
▮▮▮▮▮▮▮▮▮▮▮▮▮▮ baseball game, ▮ Gnome
▮▮▮▮▮▮▮▮▮▮▮▮▮▮▮▮▮▮▮▮▮ !!!

Dammit, one bit me!

Sincerely,
▮▮▮▮▮▮▮▮▮▮▮▮▮▮▮▮▮▮▮▮▮▮

Zombie Garden Gnome Survival on a Budget: A Helpful Guide

While I'm sure you'd all love to live the life of a world-famous Zombie Garden Gnome hunter and own all the latest high-tech Gnome-battle gear you see in your favorite Hollywood movies, the sad reality is that most people simply don't have the resources or the drive to commit to a full-time Zombie Garden Gnome–slaying lifestyle. But even if you aren't actively pursuing them, the truth is that your home can and will be overrun by the Red-Hatted Menace at any moment, and you owe it to yourself to have these essential items in your home and easily accessible at all times.

CHECKLIST

Gardening gloves	Index cards
Argyle socks	Pencils
Steel-toed boots	Paper clips
Raisins	Toilet paper
Snowblower	Thumbtacks
Rubber bands	Big floppy hat

GARDENING GLOVES

Any basic pair will protect you from Gnome bites, but if you can spring for a high-end pair, you should. It will cost a little bit more up front, but the cheaper gloves will have to be replaced after every single Zombie Garden Gnome attack. If you live in North or South America, Europe, Asia, Australia, Africa, on an island, in the Arctic, or anywhere else prone to massive, frequent zombie attacks, you'll be replacing the store-brand gloves almost daily. A few dollars more on your first trip to the store will save you a lot of driving in the terrible, terrible weeks ahead.

ARGYLE SOCKS

The taller and thicker the better. Multiple layers if you can. Some historians speculate that the argyle pattern was originally developed in Scotland in the seventeenth century for the express purpose of confusing Zombie Garden Gnomes who found themselves hypnotized by the diagonal lines and patterns, but it should be noted that those historians aren't very good at their jobs.

STEEL-TOED BOOTS

Maybe we seem hung up on footwear, but keep in mind that you're dealing with very, very short predators here. Zombie Flamingo Guides spend an inordinate amount of time on codpieces, championship belts, and chain-mail vests, but our focus here is mostly below the knees. If Zombie Garden Gnomes end up developing tiny, tiny ladder technology, rest assured that we'll take that into account in future editions of this guidebook.

RAISINS

Nature's perfect snack. They're nutritious and delicious, and life's always better with raisins. Buy ten boxes today! Or a hundred! You can never have too many raisins!

TWO-STAGE, 36-INCH, SELF-PROPELLED, INFINITELY VARIABLE, HYDROSTATIC TRACK DRIVE SNOWBLOWER WITH ELECTRIC START

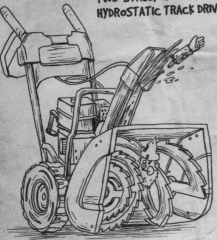

These retail for about $8,000, but you really should treat yourself. You never know when the Zombie Gnome Apocalypse will start, and do you really want to spend what could be the final moments of your life wrestling with an inferior snowblower? Top of the line all the way. You deserve it.

PENCILS
You know what we're going to say, right?

RUBBER BANDS
At least a dozen.

TOILET PAPER
Helpful hint: Buy two-ply, and you can carefully unroll it into two single-ply rolls. You'll need to start cutting your expenses a bit after that snowblower purchase.

PAPER CLIPS
Get a dozen of these, too.

THUMBTACKS
The pointier, the better.

INDEX CARDS
Not to sound like a broken record, but it would be smart to have about twelve of these in your survival kit.

BIG FLOPPY HAT
Although a big floppy hat offers little to no protection from Zombie Gnomes, sunburn is no laughing matter. You'll thank me for this later.

That settles it. Zombie Gnomes are very real and have kidnapped Dave. At first Dr. Griebel thought they'd eaten him. She took a lot of excited notes and made me search the garden for bones. Fortunately, all I found were some old zucchini, which were unpleasant but not actually man-eating.

A week later, we got the first postcard.

It seems the Zombie Gnomes are taking Dave on a cross-country tour. Dr. Griebel is very excited about this display of Gnome intelligence. I am very unexcited about Dr. Griebel's recent demand that I slather myself in barbecue sauce when I go out to get the mail. Somehow I sense that I may be next.

FROM THE CHRONICLES OF HERR RANIER VAN POORT,
ZOMBIE HUNTER: PART THE FLERFTH

[EDITOR'S NOTE: Looks like the word "Flerfth." This portion of the journal was badly torn, slightly burned, and stained with copious amounts of tobacco and elderberries.]

—— and that is how I not only survived the Zombie Gnome attack, but reorganized my toolshed. Just remember my method whenever you are confronted by the little monsters. With this brilliant and remarkably simple move, I have at last established myself in the annals of Zombie Gnome offense. Up with Van Poort! I'm off to the pretzelarium for a well-deserved round of Bavarian Salted. [EDITOR'S NOTE: The remainder of this particular passage consists of a self-portrait, which Herr Ranier has helpfully labeled "Self-Poortrait," featuring himself vanquishing the Zombie Gnomes.]

Self-Poortrait

SPECIAL EDITION OF GILLY'S GREEN THUMB GAB

LANDSCAPING AND LAND MINES

Dear Gilly,
There's no doubt about it. My neighborhood is completely infested with Zombie Gnomes. I know things are bad because the neighborhood association is finally allowing us to build structures in our yards. They won't admit what the problem is; they just say it's to "keep out pests." But not even cranky old Mr. Tiede across the street can ignore all the tattered red hats shambling by.

Long story short: I finally have permission to build some proper outdoor defenses. But where do I begin? Is a wall or a moat the better option? Is it possible to turn one's yard into a gauntlet of death traps and still have stylish landscaping?

Chloe

Dear Chloe,
Your last question is the easiest to answer. Yes, yes, yes! A Zombie Gnome Apocalypse is no excuse to sacrifice curb appeal. Allow me to present a few popular landscaping styles updated for today's gardener with subtle, attractive, anti-Gnome features. Pick the look that works with your home, or use these as inspiration to create your own unique style.

Gilly

A ZOMBIE GNOME APOCALYPSE IS NO EXCUSE TO SACRIFICE CURB APPEAL.

The Cottage Garden

Also known as the English garden, this style brings the romance of Old World village life to your home with wooden fences, enticing pathways, and sprays of colorful flowers. The cottage style is free-form so you can fill it with as few or as many Gnome traps as you please. If the piles of little bodies become unsightly, just plant more flowers!

The picket fence. Fortunately, barriers don't have to be tall to keep out a hjorde of Zombie Gnomes. They just have to be sturdy. For a fun twist on the traditional picket fence, try a row of spikes topped with the severed heads of your tiny undead victims. Now you've got a charming entranceway *and* an entertaining new collection and conversation starter.

Winding paths. As we Jane Austen fans know, it's not an English garden without a picturesque garden walk. Complement the traditional gentle, curving path with deadfalls, spike-lined pits, and land mines. Lure Zombie Gnomes onto the pathways by spraying them with the scent of blood (available online from big-game suppliers, or you can distill your own for that personal touch) and watch your hard work pay off! From a safe distance, of course. Zombie fluids can spatter.

Quaint elements. This style of garden cries out for little touches of charm. This is the place for all your antiques show finds: an old wheelbarrow, a vintage pitchfork, a few bear traps strewn casually about, a line of rusty crossbows set to rain arrows on any tiny undead that happen to wander down Rusty Crossbow Lane. For a touch of Merrie Olde England, imagine an Iron Maiden nestled cunningly among the tea roses.

The Zen Garden

Japanese garden design is simple but filled with surprises, ideal for luring the undead to their destruction. With remarkably few modifications, you can create a yard that offers both spiritual tranquility and real peace of mind.

The moat. It's hardly a Japanese-inspired garden without a water feature. Whether you populate your moat with a school of decorative piranha or simply fill it with hydrofluoric acid, it's easy to make it as beautiful as it is practical. Ferns or trailing flowers planted around the moat will add elegance while obscuring the edges, increasing the chances of Zombie Gnomes stumbling in.

Bonsai. For a little cheeky fun, cultivate tiny trees and shrubs, scaled to your knee-high intruders. Shambling through a bonsai grove, they'll look like full-size Zombies! Of course, the fun isn't complete until you add adorable Gnome-size swinging log traps.

The rock garden. A traditional Zen rock garden dovetails perfectly with contemporary anti-Gnome landscaping design. In fact, I suggest making it your focal point. Just replace the usual boring old gravel with quicksand.

The Contemporary Garden

Sleek minimalism and geometric shapes are the hallmarks of contemporary style. Modernist design, though elegant, can seem cold and uninviting if you aren't careful, so the last thing you want are a bunch of little reanimated corpses walking around making things look grim. Let's dispose of them, shall we?

High-tech elements. With a contemporary garden, you can get away with modern amenities that would look out of place in an old-fashioned cottage garden or a Zen retreat. There's no reason not to install a few deadly lasers, for instance. When they're not slicing Zombie Gnomes into tiny pieces, they can provide the kids with fabulous bedtime light shows. Electrified walkways are also a must.

The fire pit. One of the most popular landscaping elements in recent years is the outdoor fire pit. It's ideal for any family event, from romantic evenings to marshmallow roasts. It's also perfect for Zombie Gnome invasions. Do I have to list all the possibilities? Get as many fire pits as you can fit in your yard without sacrificing aesthetics and rig them to belch flame at random intervals. Invite the neighbors over for a fun-filled Gnome barbecue. Or just leave them burning and trust in the natural Zombie fear of fire to keep Zombie Gnomes away from your outdoor cocktail party.

Abstract sculpture. Nothing says modernism like a big pointy sculpture. And nothing says peace of mind like a series of big pointy sculptures, cunningly arranged to spear unwary Zombie Gnomes as they shamble along the complicated angular pathways of your garden. It's extra cool if they shoot darts.

<blockquote>
"

IT'S IDEAL FOR ANY FAMILY EVENT, FROM ROMANTIC EVENINGS TO MARSHMALLOW ROASTS. IT'S ALSO PERFECT FOR ZOMBIE GNOME INVASIONS.

"
</blockquote>

The Kitchen Garden

More and more homeowners are discovering the pleasures of practical gardening, a trend I wholeheartedly endorse. There's nothing more delicious than homegrown organic vegetables, and the ability to grow food will be in high demand should the Zombie Gnomes destroy society and thrust us into a post-apocalyptic hellscape. So all hail the kitchen gardener! If you're ready to start tilling the soil, here are ideas for a traditional vegetable garden that's attractive, practical, and anathema to the undead.

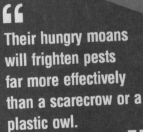

> **Their hungry moans will frighten pests far more effectively than a scarecrow or a plastic owl.**

Useful crops. It's a joy to discover the practical applications of ordinary garden plants. Peas and mint make for a refreshing spring luncheon, homegrown tomatoes are marvelous in a pasta sauce, and hot chili peppers mixed with phosphorus make an eye-scorching grenade. Plant Scottish thistle as an attractive natural substitute for barbed wire and line your deadfalls with sharpened bamboo from your own bamboo grove. Disappointingly, most organic poisons have no effect on Zombie Gnomes, but a blow dart full of ricin, which you can extract yourself from the castor oil plant, will knock them out long enough for you to collect them and put them to good use (see below).

Trellises. Once your vegetable beds are established, you'll be clamoring for more space. Trellising is an excellent way to increase your yield while keeping vegetables safe from rot and insects. Even better, sturdy steel trellises make excellent Zombie Gnome cages. Their hungry moans will frighten pests far more effectively than a scarecrow or a plastic owl. Any squirrel or rabbit foolish enough to venture into your garden will be devoured messily. You'll almost want to thank your Zombie Gnomes for being such good little guards to your squash and tomatoes. (Don't thank them, though. They'd eat your legs if they could get free.)

Composting. Leaving defeated Zombies lying around to rot is so wasteful. The mindful gardener sets up a dedicated compost bin for the undead. After eight to ten weeks (six in hot summers), you'll have rich compost for your organic vegetables. *Warning:* If the compost is moving, it's still infected with the Zombie Gnome virus. Never till the soil with compost that tries to escape.

From the Chronicles of HERR RANIER VAN POORT,
ZOMBIE HUNTER—
uncle Ranier's Rainy Day Storytime Break

Fate once more conspires against me. I had tracked a hjorde of Zombie Gnomes to one of those newfangled miniatured golfing courses outside of Pittsburgh. Such installations often attract the diminutive undead; they seem to enjoy weathered, desiccated architecture on their own scale. No sooner had I entered the grounds, however, than the very heavens opened above me. I am now curled inside a small plywood windmill, waiting out the rainstorm.

To put this time to good use, I shall endeavor to record some of the traditional tales of Zombie Gnomes from the old country. I heard many of these from my own grandmother as she sat by the fireside on a winter's night, stirring a pot of gently screaming Gnomes she'd caught in the chicken coop that morning. Although these are fanciful folktales, they contain wisdom from the Gnome-kicking ancients that may aid us today.

Snow White
and the Seven Zombie Gnomes

Once upon a time, there lived a beautiful young princess named
Snow White. Although she was loved by the people of the kingdom,
her wicked stepmother envied her beauty and grew to hate her. One
fateful day, the queen bade her royal hunter to take Snow White into
the forest and kill her. The hunter could not bring himself to perform
such a dreadful deed, so he freed Snow White to flee into the forest.

Deep in the forest, Snow White came upon a tiny, smelly cottage.
She crawled inside and, finding it empty, fell fast asleep. Soon the
seven Zombie Gnomes who lived in the little cottage came shambling
home. And then the Gnomes ate her.

Ali Baba
and the Forty Zombie Gnomes

Once upon a time, there lived a poor woodcutter named Ali Baba. One day Ali Baba was in the forest when he happened to see a hjorde of forty Zombie Gnomes shambling by. He followed them in secret, hoping they would lead him to the legendary cavern of the Zombie Gnomes. Sure enough, the Gnomes shambled up to an apparently solid cliff. When they spoke the magic word "hrrruUGHHHHurkkugh," a door opened and they lurched in.

After the door had shut, Ali Baba crept out of hiding. "HrrruUGHHHHurkkugh," he said, and the magic door opened. Thus Ali Baba entered a cavern containing forty Zombie Gnomes. And then the Gnomes ate him.

The Shoemaker
and the Zombie Gnomes

Once upon a time, a poor shoemaker despaired of being able to make enough shoes to buy bread. That night, he heard strange sounds of shuffling and moaning in his little shop. He awoke to find that all his shoes had been eaten. The shoemaker scraped together the leather and thread to make more shoes, but again something came in the night and ate every last one. After making yet another batch of shoes, the shoemaker decided to stay up all night and find out who was responsible. To his surprise, he saw a hjorde of Zombie Gnomes lurch into his shop! And then the Gnomes ate him.

Gnome in Boots

Once upon a time, a poor boy's father died, leaving him only a Zombie Gnome and a pair of sturdy boots. And then the Gnome ate him.

Goldilocks
and the Three Zombie Gnomes

Once upon a time, there was a little girl named Goldilocks. And then the Gnomes ate her.

The Boy Who Cried
Zombie Gnomes

Once upon a time, there was a mischievous shepherd boy. Bored with watching his master's sheep, he ran into the nearby village, shouting, "Zombie Gnomes! Zombie Gnomes!" The villagers armed themselves with their sharpest farm implements and their heaviest Gnome-stomping boots, only to find the boy laughing at their credulity. A few days later, the shepherd boy played the same prank. Once again, the villagers panicked, and once again the boy had a hearty laugh at their expense. Soon enough, the boy played the prank again. And then the villagers ate him and blamed it on the Zombie Gnomes.

The Gingerbread
Zombie Gnome

Once upon a time, an old woman made a Zombie Gnome out of gingerbread. The Gingerbread Zombie Gnome came to unlife and lurched out of the oven, lightly quipping, "hrrruUGHHHHurkkugh." And then the old woman ate him.

Classical Gnomeric Hymns

Although the origins of Zombie Gnomes are lost to the mists of history, prehistory, or possibly pre-prehistory (to those who believe in a time before even the dinosaurs that has not been preserved in the fossil record because Zombie Gnomes ate everything), it's certain they have had a profound impact on the arts. Few paintings and even fewer painters of Zombie Gnomes survive today, but countless* poems and songs have been written about these horrible, horrible little monsters.

The most beloved of these poems are presented here as an attempt to bring just a little culture to this waterlogged journal.

*About four.

Gnomes

by Juice Killedmore

I think that into my home
I shall invite a Garden Gnome.
A Gnome whose hungry mouth is pressed
Against the—AAAAAAAAAAAAUUUUUUUUUGGGGGHHHHH!!!

GNOME MAN IS AN ISLAND
by John Well Done

Gnome Man is an island, or is tired of an elf; every Gnome eats
to his contentment, eating parts of the man; if some arms be
gnawed—awaaaaaaaaaaaaaaarrrgghhhh!!!

THE FOOD NOT EATEN
by Robert Frosting

Two Gnomes diverged in a yellow wood,
And sorry I was chased by both
And be one meal, if long I stood
And they looked me down as one would a pork chop
or some kind of glazed ham
To where they—oh, no, oh, no, oh, please don't—aaaaaahhhh!!!

DO NOT GO GENTLE
INTO THAT GNOME'S BELLY
by Dill N. Humus

Do not go gentle into that Gnome's belly,
old age should you try to achieve,
But rage, rage sends them against thauuuuuuuuuugggghhh.

I'd hoped that Dave's kidnapping would shake Dr. Griebel out of her mania and force her to accept that we're dealing with something truly dangerous. Of course not. Dr. Griebel gets more excited with each new postcard from the Gnomes. "You realize what this means, Babs?" she says. "These apparently mindless walking corpses are, in fact, capable of advanced cognition! Perhaps they can be trained and put to productive use!"

I hate being called "Babs."

Late one night in a fit of inspiration, possibly brought on by inhaling weed-killer fumes in the lab garden, Dr. Griebel drew up a new set of plans. I found them tacked to the wall when I came in that morning.

PRACTICAL APPLICATIONS OF THE ZOMBIE GARDEN GNOME

- If it is indeed possible to train Zombie Gnomes, they could become valuable, if pungent, little garden helpers.

- Undead strength harnessed for transportation

- Can gnaw through sheetrock—home renovation a snap!

- Perfect scarecrow: Moves, groans, eats critters, smells terrible

- Chorus of piping voices delights the ear & heart
  (must learn if corpses can carry a tune)

PROBLEM: Not much grant money in gardening.
Think of something more lucrative.

THE ZOMBIE GARDEN GNOME:
MILITARY APPLICATIONS

- Drop into enemy territory for general unpleasantness
- Can be fired long-range (must test distance and aerodynamics)
- Attach explosives to Gnomes to create ambulatory land mines
- Deploy into space—they don't need to breathe!

BABS, WRITE UP A GRANT PROPOSAL. $$$!!!

I'm very concerned about the turn these plans are taking. Dr. Griebel is now in the lab trying to tie firecrackers to one of our test Gnomes. Did I mention that we have a cage full of test Gnomes? I'm not crazy about that idea, either.

AND I HATE BEING CALLED "BABS"!

My adventure in the miniatured golfing establishment ended in grim victory for the Red-Hatted Menace. Not only did the hjorde I was tracking escape after devouring the contents of the snack stand (hot-dog sausages, pommes frites, approximately five hundred small ketchup packets, mustard) and at least one ball boy (baggy trousers, acne), but in the aftermath I discovered that the rain had gotten into my satchel. My most recent notes were soaked, not to mention gnawed by the last fleeing Gnomes.

I shall lay these pages out to dry and hope they emerge in readable condition. Pray for them, Dear Reader, for your own survival depends upon my notes! And it would be a pain in the neck to have to write all this out again.

Zombie Gnomes:
Regional Variations

To my eternal consternation, Zombie Gnomes have spread almost everywhere on the globe. Despite their limited brainpower, the creatures have gradually adapted to incredibly varied environments. As a young Zombie Gnome hunter, callow fool that I was, I thought fighting Gnomes would be much the same everywhere. I learned my lesson the hard way in the swamps of Louisiana, tracking a new hjorde. I was waist-deep in water when all around me the swamp began to bubble, and without warning there arose [illegible] [illegible] barely escaped with my [illegible] covered in a delicious brown sugar marinade.

Don't let the same thing happen to you! Study these examples of regional Zombie Gnomes.

The Country Zombie Gnome

Zombie Gnomes thrive in rural farmland, where they find ample hiding places, extensive lurching ground, and plenty of live meat on the hoof. Once established, a hjorde can wreak havoc, destroying livestock and devouring farmers with equal relish. A Zombie Gnome is capable of skeletonizing a cow in a matter of minutes, and several Gnomes together may even [illegible] [illegible] fishing chunks out of the river for weeks.

Fortunately, farm families in areas infested with Zombie Gnomes soon learn to treat them like any other pest. Heavy-duty agricultural equipment is ideal for chopping up a hungry hjorde. But keeping the countryside free of Zombie Gnomes requires constant vigilance. I know of a large factory farm that lost an entire herd of cattle to a hjorde that got past its lax security. Somehow the farm was able to fill its quota of ground beef anyway, although customers complained about biting down on tiny beards. This is one of the eight reasons I never eat hamburgers.

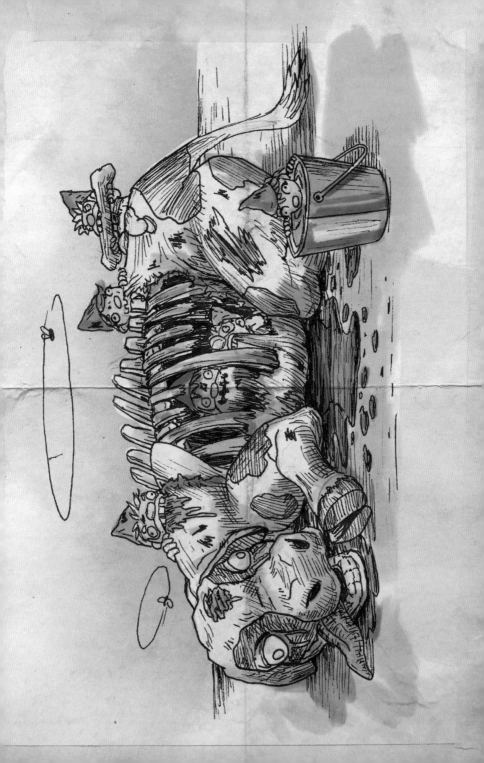

The Urban Zombie Gnome

Like rats, pigeons, and ninja turtles, Urban Zombie Gnomes are capable of surviving, even thriving, in the dank corners of modern cities. These are among the wiliest of the Zombie Gnomes, adept at hiding from humans and evading traps. Zombie Gnome hunters will find their skills tested to their full extent when tracking a city hjorde.

Urban Zombie Gnomes often take up residence in sewers and subway tunnels. Entire sections of the New York subway line had to be boarded up permanently after the Manhattan Thing We Don't Talk About of 1984. This disaster began when a hjorde was attracted to a cheeseburger abandoned in a subway car on 42nd Street and quickly [illegible] sprayed as high as fifteen feet on the walls [illegible] rather than hosing off the mess, elected to give up and close the line down. But everything past Lincoln Center is probably safe by now.

From my personal experience with this elusive breed of Zombie Gnome, I can only say this: If a taxi pulls up and it seems at all possible that the driver is several tiny people in a coat, absolutely *do not* get in.

The House Zombie Gnome

The typical House Zombie Gnome is not what one would call "sneaky." The sounds of shuffling and devouring can be heard up to a quarter-mile away, and the smell carries much farther. Some hjordes, however, have learned to live quietly in human homes. They most often take up residence in the walls, although they have been known to congregate in little-used cellars, attics, and, on at least one occasion I was unfortunate enough to witness, a septic tank.

Residents may notice tiny footprints and bite marks in the house, and food and pets may go missing. But, for the most part, House Zombie Gnomes are unobtrusive guests. Their hosts may easily be lulled into a false sense of security, even finding the occasional sign of wee folk charming. Until, that is, the inevitable day when the walls fill up with tiny freeloading corpses and they burst out into the sitting room, hungry and twitching with pent-up energy.

The Desert Zombie Gnome

Unlike the elusive Dessert Zombie Gnome, which frequents bakeries and malt shops, the Desert Zombie Gnome enjoys arid climates, such as the American Southwest, North Africa, and automobiles with broken air-conditioning systems. On one occasion, I came across an entire nest of them lounging in a particularly dry Thanksgiving turkey prepared by my Aunt Helga, but fortunately I was able to dispatch them with three-and-a-half cans of cranberry sauce.

Due to that incident, I never travel anywhere without at least four cans of cranberry sauce. A small lighter or book of matches is also helpful, as the Desert Zombie Gnomes are highly susceptible to open flames. In the event that you don't encounter any Desert Zombie Gnomes on your next visit to Arizona, you can always win friends by offering to cook them up a nice can of warm cranberry sauce.

The Northern Zombie Gnome

Originating in Siberia, this is one of the oldest and hardiest
varieties of Zombie Gnome. Cold does not bother the undead. In
fact, it provides a useful "refrigeration" effect, allowing the horrible
things to keep lurching through the permafrost almost indefinitely.
There are even cases of Northern Zombie Gnomes freezing
completely for years, only to thaw out and immediately leap for the
nearest juicy pair of kneecaps. That's why it's imperative for you to
check a bag of party ice thoroughly before opening.

   In some snowbound areas, the Northern Zombie Gnome is so
common that villagers periodically try to tame them and teach them
simple tasks. Noting their unholy strength, these villagers often
train their household Zombie Gnomes to pull sledges across the
ice. This generally ceases to seem like a good idea the first time
a sled team breaks free of its harness and invariably [illegible]
[illegible] haven't been able to eat a bite of poutine since.

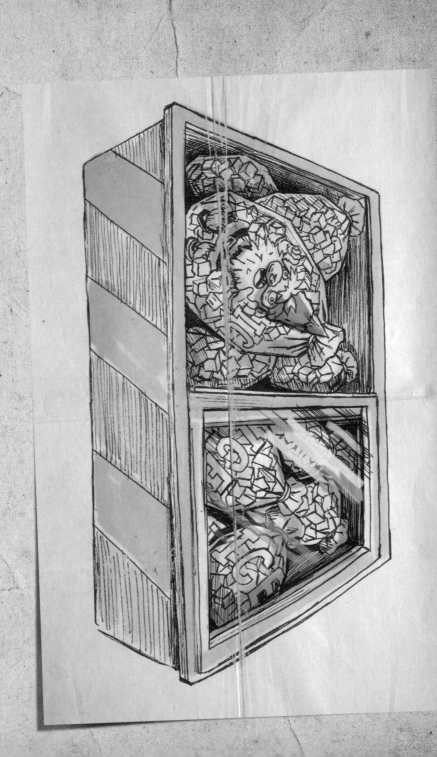

The Aquatic Zombie Gnome

Water is not kind to corpses, but since when have the undead cared about maintaining a proper skin-care regimen? Zombie Gnomes are capable of unliving underwater for a shockingly long time before rotting away.

In the 1950s, an entrepreneur with a gung-ho attitude and a deep hatred for humanity hit upon the idea of selling Zombie Gnomes as aquarium pets. Under the trademarked name Davey Jones's Incredible Sea Nasties™, mail-order Aquatic Zombie Gnomes were sold by the hundreds of thousands. Many of those who were children at the time recall ordering a Sea Nasty of their very own from the back pages of a comic book. Or they would recall it, if any of them had survived.

The Redwood Zombie Gnome

New World Zombie Gnomes have adapted with disturbing acuity to their environments. In the Pacific Northwest, for example, giant redwoods and sequoias have been colonized by a new breed of arboreal undead. Redwood Zombie Gnomes are adept if slow-paced climbers, gradually working their way to the treetops and devouring everything in their vertical path. Possessed of strong jaws, even by Zombie Gnome standards, they gnaw nests for themselves in tree trunks, from which they can reach out and grab passing birds and squirrels. Mounds of tiny bones piled around the foot of a redwood tree are a sure sign of infestation.

As the Redwood Zombie Gnome inhabits treetops deep in the woods, one might imagine that at least this breed isn't dangerous to humans. In fact, however, Redwood Zombie Gnomes seem specifically adapted to hunt and devour hippies and environmentalists who climb the trees to commune with nature, or whatever it is those folks get up to. Many a nature lover has vanished into Yosemite, leaving behind only a bloody do-rag and perhaps a beard.

Camping in the majestic redwood forest thus joins the long list of things the Zombie Gnomes have ruined for humanity, along with hobby aquariums, taxicabs, midnight foosball, rock gardening, plant gardening, really any kind of gardening whatsoever, septic tanks [illegible] hamburgers, [illegible] [illegible] and that, Dear Reader, is reason number six.

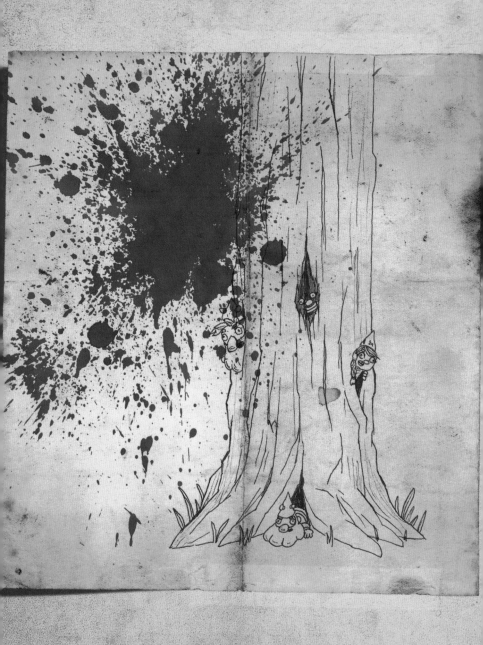

To the layperson, Zombie Gnomes appear to be simple forest sprites with simple needs. But as a seasoned expert like myself can attest, even a novice, completely untrained Zombie Gnome enthusiast can spend a lifetime studying these fascinating creatures. A short, terrible, pain-filled, excruciatingly awful lifetime, to be sure, but a lifetime nonetheless. Perhaps I shouldn't have sent so many woefully incompetent people into direct contact with the Red-Hatted Menace, but thanks to the efforts of these brave, brave, brave (and, to be brutally honest, dead, dead, dead) individuals, I have compiled a comprehensive field guide to these awful, awful, awful (did I mention awful?) little monsters.

While I would like to say that the information contained in this section has been painstakingly fact-checked by an expert team of Zombie Gnome experts, I'm going to be honest here and admit that, due to my own globe-trotting efforts and a very busy summer on the Zombie Gnome lecture circuit, I have not been able to verify all their research firsthand.

Most of the information here has been compiled from remnants of bloodstained field journals, and, as you can imagine, one's penmanship tends to suffer greatly when one is being torn limb from limb by a rampaging hjorde of Zombie Gnomes. Although most of my guesses fall into the "educated" category, some of these measurements are, to be very generous, "way the heck off" or "grossly incompetent," if I'm being totally honest.

If you are unfortunate enough to encounter Zombie Gnomes in the wild and find that any of these notations are in error, please send any corrections to my attention courtesy of my publisher, and I shall do my best to express my utmost gratitude to your next of kin. (Perhaps a nice fruit basket or floral arrangement. Something simple, yet tasteful.)

MEASURE OF A MENACE

HEIGHT

Oh, let's just say it's around twelve inches, plus or minus a red, pointy hat. A standard Garden Gnome statue may be as tall as twenty-four inches, but please be advised that these are primarily displayed in some misguided attempt to keep Zombie Gnomes from invading one's home.

I can't stress enough that this method of Zombie Gnome repellent doesn't work. If anything, an oversized Garden Gnome displayed in your front yard is going to attract even more Zombie Gnomes than an unadorned lawn. The only proven deterrent is no yard at all, or, better yet, plastic explosive lawn flamingoes. While this also wards off squirrels, butterflies, paperboys, rain, and just about everything in general, cleanup is incredibly difficult. Invest in a good tarp if you go this route. Oh, and maybe I'll upgrade that first answer to twelve-and-a-half inches, so it sounds less like a number that a tearful Zombie Gnome hunter just made up on the spot.

WEIGHT

The standard Zombie Gnome is surprisingly dense, and not in that "prefers the movie adaptation to the original novel" sort of way. Although their standing height is a mere twelve-and-a-half inches (see previous entry—would I lie to you?), a Zombie Gnome weighs nearly fourteen pounds, roughly as much as a standard bowling ball.

While fourteen pounds may not sound like a lot, try throwing a bowling ball at your best friend sometime and you'll get a sense of just how much damage a Zombie Gnome can do when he drops down on you from a shadowy bookshelf or a pine tree.

TEETH

A healthy Garden Gnome has a full set of thirty-two teeth upon reaching maturity, but Zombie Gnomes are, by definition, not healthy (and not all that mature, if their Twitter account is any indication). One plucky (now deceased) member of our research team once documented as many as five teeth in a Zombie Gnome's mouth, but that didn't work out so well for him (or anyone involved). Let's just go with "fewer than thirty-two" and hope that you'll never find out for yourself.

CLAWS

Sooooooo sharp. A Zombie Gnome's fingernails are less than a half-centimeter in length, but they can carve through granite like a hot knife through butter. When their fingernails are dull, their clawing prowess is not unlike a room-temperature knife through a butter substitute that was only recently removed from the fridge. If their nails are broken entirely, we suggest throwing a stick of butter at them, or, alternatively, greasing the soles of your feet with butter to facilitate a speedy departure. For more information about butter, please consult your local library or dairy farm.

DIET

Like traditional Garden Gnomes, Zombie Gnomes have been known to spend the afternoon meticulously gathering acorns and carefully arranging them on decorative leaves.

Unlike traditional Garden Gnomes, who opt to quietly nibble on their stash of acorns, the Zombie Gnomes use them as projectiles to be hurled at their actual food of choice, literally anything that moves. They've been known to devour small rodents, pets, and all manner of woodland creatures, but they show a strong preference for humans, as they are easily distracted, lack claws, and, let's be honest, have very poor survival instincts.

SENSES

If you're not just skimming this book (and you shouldn't—your survival depends on it!), then you'll note our mention of humanity's "very poor survival instincts." It's impossible to quantify the senses of the Zombie Gnome, but we do know that every single one of their senses is more acute than our own. They can see better than us, they can hear better than us, and they can smell us from miles away.

Although I had hoped to conduct some experiments to determine the limits of a Zombie Gnome's sense of taste, the scientific community really, really frowns upon capturing different sizes and shapes of people and dropping them into large holes filled with hungry Zombie Gnomes, even if it's for science and even if you've gotten them to sign waivers and everything.

LIFE SPAN

The natural life span of a Garden Gnome has been estimated at over four hundred years, which means that a Gnome who was already an adult when the United States declared its independence from Britain still has another century to go before he needs to start looking into post-retirement hobbies.

It's still unclear whether the zombification process will greatly lengthen or greatly reduce the longevity of Gnomes, and this has been the subject of intense debate among ~~weirdos on the internet~~ respected Gnome scientists. One school of thought says that a Zombie Gnome deprived of food would only survive for two hundred years on its own, while other scientists feel that a Zombie Gnome is effectively immortal, for all intents and purposes. As the typical Zombie Gnome research scientist's life span is much, much, much shorter than that of literally any other type of research scientists (even the scientists who study the effects of dynamite and alcohol on laser-powered cobras), it may be another seven hundred years before we have conclusive results on this.

FAMILIAL RELATIONSHIPS

Garden Gnomes mate for life, and, barring extraordinary ecological upheaval, tend to live within a three-mile radius of their entire extended family. Zombie Gnomes, in contrast, tend to be solitary creatures, but they make up for this by eating entire extended families whenever possible.

When buying a home, ALWAYS make sure that your realtor discloses its proximity to the nearest Garden Gnome village. Anything within ten miles (hitchhiking distance) is considered high-risk, but anything fewer than two miles (Zombie Gnome catapult distance) falls into the might-as-well-cover-yourself-in-barbecue-sauce-every-morning category.

OFFSPRING/REPRODUCTION

The Zombie Gnome population replenishes itself through regular attacks on humanity and on uninfected Garden Gnomes. The Zombie Gnome plague seems to be spread primarily through biting, clawing, and the "spearing" method, in which a Zombie Gnome's hat punctures an unsuspecting victim.

In a groundbreaking 2007 study, noted Zombie Gnome expert Dr. George Peterson claimed that he had surreptitiously witnessed a Zombie Gnome mating ritual, wherein the male Zombie Gnome serenaded a female with a beautiful doo-wop-style ballad, followed by a romantic candlelight dinner, but it should be noted that Dr. Peterson is kind of a weirdo.

DAILY ROUTINE: Unlike their non-monstrous brethren, Zombie Gnomes have no discernible schedule or routine. They show a slight preference for nighttime feedings, but are largely unaffected by sunlight, seasonal changes, or any sort of extreme weather.

Zombie Gnomes maintain small homes, often furnished with rooms that remind them of their pre-Zombie lives, but these homes serve a nostalgic purpose, not a practical one, since the Gnomes themselves have little to no need for rest or shelter.

No amount of food can ever satiate a Zombie Gnome, so their meals are unscheduled and unplanned. No amount of rest will make a Zombie Gnome more awake or alert, so they maintain nothing resembling a traditional sleep cycle.

They are nomadic and irritable, and you would do best to avoid them every time of day, but be advised that they seem most hungry at dusk.

HANDICRAFTS

For centuries, human visitors have enjoyed the quaint charm of Gnome handicrafts, from beard-scented candles to tiny shoes, decorative baskets, and beautiful, lovingly assembled birdhouses.

Zombie Gnome handicrafts, though, are mostly made of discarded hands. Why they take this term so literally is a subject of serious debate among Zombie Gnome scholars. For further reading on this matter, please consult the fine Zombie Gnome journals of Dr. Henry "Lefty" Harrison, Dr. Emily "Lefty" Sanchez, and Dr. Eleanor "Lefty" O'Donnell.

RELATIONS WITH ANIMALS

Traditional Gnomes are completely at harmony with nature and have a kinship with all forest animals. Zombie Gnomes, on the other hand, will eat anything they can catch.

The standard North American raccoon is the only animal that seems to instill fear in Zombie Gnomes. Their speed, dexterity, claws, and unpredictability make them more trouble than they're worth for a Zombie Gnome hoping to score a quick meal, so the two factions have developed an uneasy accord.

One (obviously) now-deceased scientist dressed himself in a suit made of live raccoons to attempt the most up-close study of Zombie Gnomes to date, but the Zombie Gnomes not only weren't fooled, but were so insulted that they formed an alliance with the raccoons and made quick work of the aforementioned scientist, Dr. Henry "Lefty" Harrison.

GAMES

Nearly all the "games" that Zombie Gnomes play are "playful" methods of eating their prey. Their favorite game could be compared to bowling, if bowling involved severed body parts, pointy hats, and comfortable footwear.

LANGUAGE

Imagine a mild, spring day. The gentle breeze smells faintly of wildflowers and carries with it the melodious sound of crickets. A songbird calls to its mate, and you'd almost swear that you can hear the sound of a butterfly's wings gently flapping.

The language of the Zombie Gnomes is the exact opposite of all that. Thrash metal played by an angry guitarist who hates music and is covered in bees. A bear with the stomach flu forced to ride a broken roller coaster in 110-degree weather while wearing an asbestos topcoat. A bucketful of wolverines fighting over the first scrap of food they've seen in three days.

There is nothing sweet, melodic, or remotely enjoyable about the Zombie Gnome language. But be advised that if you do hear them, it's already too late, since their horrible, horrible vocalizations are always a prelude to their dinner.

STRENGTH

While Zombie Gnomes aren't especially strong, they make up for that deficiency through sheer tenacity. A single Zombie Gnome couldn't uproot a tree, for example, but four or five of them working together will gladly spend weeks gnawing through an oak tree until they topple it.

One Zombie Gnome can't pull down an adult human by himself, but two or three of them working in conjunction can cause even the most sure-footed person to take a tumble.

I have seen film footage depicting Zombie Gnomes ripping full-sized phone books in half, but, to the best of my knowledge, this is more of a party trick than a feat of strength.

WEATHER PREDICTIONS

Standard Gnomes are known for their weather-predicting abilities, and Zombie Gnomes are too, in their own inimitable manner.

When rain is imminent, Zombie Gnomes will scurry around and devour everything in their path.

When snow is on its way, Zombie Gnomes will scurry around and devour everything in their path.

When the weather is about to undergo a massive, sudden change, Zombie Gnomes will scurry around and devour everything in their path.

When stability is the forecast, Zombie Gnomes will scurry around and devour everything in their path.

TOOLS

Standard Gnomes are master builders. They forge their own tiny tools and take great pride in their construction projects and handicrafts. Zombie Gnomes' use of tools is limited to bludgeoning people and animals with their own severed limbs, and we must admit this "tool usage" seems more accidental than deliberate.

Editor's note: Upon fact-checking this section, we learned that „GnomeCore" is a popular genre in Scandinavian countries, and it makes up an astonishing 85 percent of their music industry.

SONGS OF THE ZOMBIE GNOMES

See the earlier "Language" section. An infinite number of producers using an infinite number of Autotune programs would still not be able to find anything melodic about the "songs" of the Zombie Gnomes.

CONTAGION, SPREAD OF:

The Zombie Gnome plague is spread primarily through the bite of the Zombie Gnome. Ordinary, delightful Garden Gnomes bitten by Zombie Gnomes will become small, horrible, walking corpses within forty-eight hours. It is speculated that the virus could also be spread by Garden Gnomes' favorite gesture of affection—rubbing noses—but Zombie Gnomes just bite noses clean off anyway.

Zombie Gnome bites are usually fatal to humans, or at least very itchy. On rare occasions, victims instead develop symptoms of Gnome Zombification, or Gnecrosis. In these cases, the infected human grows a long white beard, seeks shelter in hollow trees and cozy riverbanks, and, in the final stages, starts chewing on other people's kneecaps. There is no known cure.

HISTORICAL BACKGROUND

The Zombie Gnome outbreak seems to have originated in Bavaria in the nineteenth century. The plague gradually spread across mainland Europe in the early twentieth century, and by the 1970s, Zombie Gnomes had spread their contagion worldwide.

The worldwide rise in the population of Zombie Gnomes seems to correlate directly with the rise of disco music, the pet rock, and CB radios, but that may be a simple coincidence.

GEOGRAPHICAL RANGE

Zombie Gnomes thrive in any environment that can support small, defenseless animals. While they don't seem to like snowy climates, they're willing to tough it out.

DRESS

Zombie Gnomes won't go anywhere without their trademark pointy red cap, torn blue shirt, tiny belt, and whatever remains of their shoes. While it may be possible to contain a Zombie Gnome outbreak by talking them through the forest and removing and meticulously hiding their caps and any other articles of clothing that you find, we feel that we should mention that it may be possible to eat an entire airplane using only a plastic fork and some mustard, but that doesn't mean it's a good idea.

OTHER TWILIGHT AND NIGHT BEINGS

The world is populated by many wonderful, magical enchanted rascals, ranging from benevolent helpers of children to mischievous trickster spirits.

   The following list explains the relationship between each of these fantastical beings and the Zombie Gnomes. We suggest you bookmark this page, as it will be most helpful in your travels.

   ELVES: Zombie Gnomes will eat them.

   GOBLINS: Zombie Gnomes will eat them.

   HOUSE GHOSTS: Zombie Gnomes will unsuccessfully try to eat them, but will eventually settle for eating anyone frightened by the house ghosts.

   TROLLS: Zombie Gnomes will eat them.

   DWARFS: Zombie Gnomes will eat them.

   RIVER SPIRITS: Zombie Gnomes would like to eat them, but instinctively realize that river spirits are more trouble than they're worth.

   WOOD NYMPHS: You bet that Zombie Gnomes will eat them.

   MOUNTAIN NYMPHS: Zombie Gnomes will eat them, but only in months that end with the letter "r." Plan your camping trips around this fact.

   ULDRAS: We aren't quite sure what these are, but Zombie Gnomes will eat them.

FOREIGN NAMES AND ALIASES:

Rest assured, wherever your travels may take you, Zombie Gnomes will find you.

Each nation has its own unique name for these pests. Commit this list to memory so that you can avoid hostels, pubs, and tourist attractions that are overrun by Zombie Gnomes. We've provided a rough translation for each phrase.

BELGIUM: Kleinmannekenefaceneater
(small man who eats your face)

HOLLAND: Kabouterbiterbiter (biter of Gnomes)

GERMANY: Heinzelmännchen Esser der Gesichter
(hedgehog eater of faces)

NORWAY: Biter av ankler
(ankle biter)

SWEDEN: Tuggar på huvudet
(chews on the head)

POLAND: Gnom gnom gnom
(untranslatable)

BULGARIA: Хамстер боец
(hamster fighter)

ITALY: cameriere francese
(french houseguest)

FRANCE: Interniste italien
(Italian houseguest)

IRELAND: Guy beag marbh
(little dead guy)

FINLAND: Metsä vihainen mies kasvoillesi
(angry forest man of the face)

RUSSIA: кроweчнbin' человек ест тво -n- ног-n-
(tiny man who eats your feet)

SERBIA: опаф човека цpвеног wew-n-pa
(olaf the red hat man)

CZECHOSLOVAKIA: Ten chlap není dobrý chlap
(this guy is not a good guy)

KENYA:
Mtu asiyekubaliwa
(uninvited tree man)

HUNGARY: Viseljen nehéz csizmát
(wears heavy boots)

SAMOA: faamolemole ava nei e ai lo'u vae
(please do not eat my leg)

ICELAND: Við erum öll út af döggum
(we are all out of badgers)

WALES: Bwyta stêc drwg (eater of the bad steak)

HAWAII: Pō'ino maika'i (bad guest)

KOREA: 버섯 정복 (mushroom conquest)

MALTA: Il-gnome li huwa gnome ħażin
(the Gnome that is a bad Gnome)

PORTUGAL: Quem o com o pequeno e cheira mal
(the man who is small and smells bad)

INDONESIA: Sarapan anjing (dog's breakfast)

ALBANIA: Zvarrit atë tani (squish it now)

Gnomenclature

*If you were to stack all the world's Zombie Gnomes end to end, you would immediately regret it.

*The world's fastest Zombie Gnome is also the world's tallest. The world's shortest Zombie Gnome, however, has no other distinguishing traits, which is somewhat disappointing.

*Novelty songwriter Bjern Floogleman released the single "Zombie Gnome Christmas" in December 1972, and it's still the top-selling Zombie Gnome song of all time, with over fourteen copies sold.

*There are no Zombie Gnomes in Nome, Alaska. The town of No-Gnomes-Here, Wyoming, however, is lousy with them.

*Although Zombie Gnomes reach maturity at the age of seven, their humor consists mostly of toilet jokes well into adulthood.

*Panama is the only country on Earth populated entirely by Zombie Gnomes.

*Disappointingly, famed linguist Noam Chomsky has written exactly zero guidebooks on the subject of defending yourself from Zombie Gnome attacks.

*Nearly half of all Zombie Gnomes would be 49 percent of them.

* The first Zombie Gnome president, Elbridge Gerry, is noteworthy because he was neither a Zombie, a Gnome, nor a president.

* Although they have no known dietary restrictions, when given the choice, Zombie Gnomes prefer to eat vegetarians.

*Scientists have detected almost no brain function whatsoever in Zombie Gnomes. Oddly enough, this does not disqualify them from holding public office.

*Zombie Gnome-Con is held in beautiful Muncie, Indiana, every winter. Thousands of Zombie Gnome fans from around the world gather at this annual celebration of Zombie Gnome heritage and culture, and by the end of the four-day festival, every single attendee has been eaten alive.

*The red color of the Zombie Gnome's hat symbolizes the blood of its prey. The blue color of the Zombie Gnome's shirt also symbolizes the blood of its prey, since Zombie Gnomes are completely color-blind and are almost always covered in blood.

*Legend has it that a Zombie Gnome's beard has restorative properties, although it's almost certainly a healthier decision in the long run to avoid pulling on a Zombie Gnome's beard.

*The most common Zombie Gnome surname is Auuuurrruuuurrrrrrrauuuugh, according to the last United States census.

*The Zombie Gnome's natural enemies include housecats, iguanas, mountain goats, and the late singer-songwriter John Denver.

* Each fall, rare "Pumpkin Spice" Zombie Gnomes emerge from hiding and unleash themselves on the unsuspecting populace. They always disappear by late November, when the elusive "Peppermint" Zombie Gnomes take their place.

* "The only thing we have to fear is fear itself. And Zombie Gnomes. Man, oh man, should we fear Zombie Gnomes."—Quote attributed to shoeshine boy Franklin Delagnome Roosevelt, 1935

* While it's not true that the Great Wall of China is the only structure that can be seen from space, the Great Zombie Gnome hedge maze in Scranton is the only structure that can be smelled from space.

* Swildon College in Oregon was the first university in America to offer a course in raising and educating Zombie Gnomes.

* Swildon College in Oregon was the first university in America to have its entire student population eaten by Zombie Gnomes.

* A Zombie Gnome's top running speed is roughly two miles per hour. A Zombie Gnome's top "spearing" speed can approach sixty miles per hour.

* The common Zombie Gnome hates being called "the common Zombie Gnome," and feels that every Zombie Gnome is special in its own horrible, horrible way.

Dr. Griebel is out of town meeting with some "angel investors" who are interested in funding her Zombie Gnome military project. From what I've seen of their videoconferences, the angels are very large, very scarred men in uniforms from no military I recognize. I admit I'm not up-to-date on all the militaries out there, but this may be the worst in what is turning out to be a long series of very bad ideas.

It's been a while since we received any word of Dave. This is probably not a great development, either.

Still searching for more information about the creatures. (The Zombie Gnomes, not Dr. Griebel and her new friends. Though maybe them, too.) Could there be something to that Van Poort guy and his rants? He was right about wearing thick socks. After several dead ends, I managed to track down Van Poort's "book" on Zombie Gnome defense. "Book" is in quotes because it's a stack of blue mimeographed pages held together with staples and binder clips, and several pages are brochures for a timeshare in Florida I think Van Poort is trying to unload. This is going to be a long, difficult read.

Meanwhile, I've been left to lab-sit while Dr. Griebel is out. She assigned me the nerve-racking task of cleaning up the lab garden, which is littered with decayed body parts and little pointy hats, not to mention in need of serious weeding. Fortunately, there don't seem to be many Gnomes lurching underfoot lately. Maybe the doctor's unhinged experiments had one positive side effect: Zombie Gnomes have learned to avoid the heck out of our lab.

Cleaning out a shed that had been infested with Zombie Gnomes before Dr. Griebel tested some fairly effective anti-Gnome drones on the colony (effective, at least, until another colony figured out how to launch themselves onto the drones, hijack them, and fly around chomping everything in their path, and the less said about that Tuesday the better), I found something strange. Under a flowerpot was a tiny book. Examining it closely, I saw it was made of scrap paper from Dr. Griebel's office, crudly stapled between covers made from some kind of leather. I don't know what kind of leather, exactly. I'd rather not know.

Scratched into the cover are the words THE ZOMBIII NOM DFENS GIDE.

ZOMBIII NOM
DFENS GIDE

I've copied a few pages. Whoever may someday read this journal, your guess is as good as mine.

HELLO! THIS VERY USEFUL GIDE TO
DEFNS AGAINS YUMENS. YUMENS BIG.
YUMENS STOMPY. BIG SHOOS,
HEVY BOOTS! HATE YUMENS!

BUUUUT.

YUMENS VERY TASTY.

YU LEARN DFENS AGAINS YUMANS.
NOT BE STOMPED. EAT WELL. GOOD
FOR YU! HORRAY.

DIEAGRAM OF HORIBLE DELISHUS YUMAN.

HITE: TOO BIG TO REACH TASTEE HED.
MUST EAT LEGS FURST AND WERK UP.
BOO.

WATE: VERY HEVY, VERY HARD
STOMPS WITH BIG YUMAN SHOOS.
HATE HEVY YUMAN STOMPS.

SMELLS LIKE TASTY DELISHUS.
MOST TASTY SMELL PART IS
BRANE, BUT SO HI! SO HARD TO
REECH AND CHOMP!

MOUTH ALWAYS YELING. "WHAT
THAT THING? RUN! IT BITE!
WHERE CHUNKS OF MY BODEE GO?
WAH WAH WAH." SO LOUD. BOO.

NO BEARD. SO UGLY NOT HAVING
BEARD. NOM BEARDS PRETTY.
YAY NOMS!

CLOTHING STICKS IN TEETHS.

STOMPY SHOOS WE HATES.

NOW WE TALK ABOUT HORIBLE
BAD YUMAN WEPONS AGAINS
NOMS. THIS OUR TIME TO SHARE
VERY SPESHUL ADVANS SEKRIT
TEKNEEKS FOR TO STOP EVERY
KIND OF YUMAN WEPON. YU
REMEMBER AND STOP YUMAN
ATTAKS WITH OUR SUPER
SMART STRATAJEE STRATA
STRATATATA PLANS.

PLAN FOR TO STOP GARDEN GLOVS:
EAT GARDEN GLOVS.

PLAN FOR TO STOP THIK SOKKS
WHAT STICKS IN TEETHS:
EAT SOKKS WHAT STICKS IN TEETHS.

PLAN FOR TO STOP HURTY STEEL
TOE BOOTS:
SMART STEEL. EAT BOOTS.

PLAN FOR TO STOP RAISUNS:
EAT RAISUNS. THEY NATURS
CANDEE.

PLAN FOR TO STOP RUBER BANDS,
PAPUR CLIPS, INDEKS CARDS,
PENSILLS:
JEST EAT WHOLE YUMAN OFFICE.
MUCH FASTER.

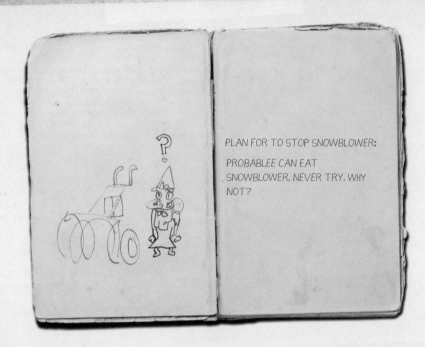

PLAN FOR TO STOP SNOWBLOWER:

PROBABLEE CAN EAT
SNOWBLOWER. NEVER TRY. WHY
NOT?

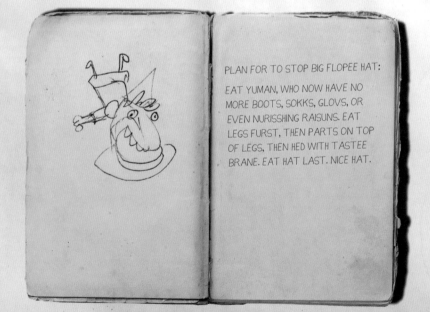

PLAN FOR TO STOP BIG FLOPEE HAT:

EAT YUMAN, WHO NOW HAVE NO
MORE BOOTS, SOKKS, GLOVS, OR
EVEN NURISSHING RAISUNS. EAT
LEGS FURST, THEN PARTS ON TOP
OF LEGS, THEN HED WITH TASTEE
BRANE. EAT HAT LAST. NICE HAT.

HAPPY STOREE TALES FROM OLDUN
TIMES FOR RAINEE DAY

THESE VERY OLD WISE FOLKSY
STOREES TOLD BY OLDEST NOMS TO
YUNG FRESH-DEAD NOMS. WIMSICAL
TALES FOR YUNG! BE HAPPY! NOMS!

TALE OF NOM AND YUMAN

ONCE ON TIME THERE NOM AND THERE
YUMAN. BITE BITE BITE BITE CHOMP
CHOMP YUM YUM YUM CHOMP. NO MORE
YUMAN! HA! HA!

THE END.

TALE OF YUMAN AND NOM

AKCHULLY, THIS ZACTLY SAME AS TALE OF
NOM AND YUMAN. NOW WE THINK IT OVER,
ALL NOM TALES ARE SAME TALE. WHY
NOT? IS GOOD TALE! YAY FOR NOMS!

Halloween Hijinks and October Surprises

Dear Gilly,

Fall is my favorite gardening season, and this year I decided to make it extra special. After canning tomato jam with the help of your classic recipe ("You Say Tomato, I Say Tomatoes, Tomatoes, Tomatoes!!!"), I went through your old October columns to collect ideas for creative Halloween decorating. What fun! I'm writing to ask whether you still recommend making centerpieces with traditional decorative corn-cobs or trendy new breeds like Glass Gem, Painted Mountain, or—I'm sorry, I can't stay perky another moment. I'm so scared. The Zombie Gnomes are everywhere. I shook

one out of my gardening boot this morning. I only escaped because it stopped to eat the boot. How can I celebrate Halloween when the dead themselves have risen and are ruining my chrysanthemums? I just can't garden anymore.

I hear their tiny footsteps on my reclaimed granite patio flagstones. Help me. . . .

Elena

Dear Elena,

Well. This has gone on long enough. The Zombie Gnomes may devour pets, bite off limbs, infect the living with their foulness, and occasion-ally clog my new acid moat with

their pesky little corpses. But when they ruin the pleasures of garden-ing, they've gone too far.

I hereby declare my impecca-bly landscaped and ridiculously well-fortified (against the Gnomes, but also rabbits and powdery mil-dew) Connecticut colonial home ground zero in the Battle against the Zombie Gnomes, and myself General of the Gnome War. Come to me, my gardeners! Arm your-selves with rake and chain saw! The wee undead will rue the day they dared leave tiny footprints in our decorative groundcover.

Gilly

Dear Gilly,
I'm a landscaper at a popular theme park/licensed property destination I'm contractually restricted from identifying by name. Lately, the place has become infested with Zombie Gnomes. The staff has tried to disguise the problem by dressing them in tiny costumes and passing them off as dwarves and friendly cartoon characters.

Last night, however, they ate the floral clock I'd been tending all year. And a churro stand. And two people working at the churro stand. But mostly the floral clock.

Should I continue to practice defensive gardening to protect the park, or is it time to get offensive?

Priyanka

P.S. We also found a guy named Dave tied up and dangling from the model Eiffel Tower in one of our popular musical-doll-based rides. He seems all right except that he can't stop humming the theme song.

Dear Priyanka,
Offend away. Offend with *fire*. And send Dave to me. I shall train him as a warrior, and possibly as my concubine. Our army grows strong and fat with vengeance.

Gilly

P.S. But don't forget to winterize your vegetable beds, folks!

With heavy heart I take leave of you, faithful and presumably not-yet-devoured reader. To these pages I have committed all my knowledge from a lifetime of hunting the Zombie Garden Gnome. It has been a difficult life, replete with ankle injuries and hours spent digging bits of undead Gnomes out of the soles of my boots. On reflection, I should have applied for that job at the pretzel factory.

Tonight the Zombie Gnomes ate my last box of raisins. For me, this is the last straw. In the morning I shall make haste to the Florida coast, where I own a timeshare (the mocking souvenir of another failed mission, during which I tracked a group of black-market Zombie Gnome dealers to the Carnation Room of a Barcelona hotel, then accidentally entered the Bougainvillea Room instead and was trapped for six hours in a presentation I could only escape by signing the deed to a condo in Fort Myers; but I digress). From this moment forward, Ranier Van Poort is retired.

Retired, you hear me?

I regret that despite learning more than any living man or Gnome on the subject of defense against the Zombie Gnomes, I never discovered an offensive weapon capable of turning the tide against the tiny, gnashy-toothed invaders. Reader: Wear thick socks, remember your G.N.O.M.E.s, and if you try to look me up, I'll shoot you on sight.

I've been in Florida for a week and I'm out of retirement. I, Ranier Van Poort, have discovered the ultimate weapon against Zombie Garden Gnomes. It began with a startling realization: *Florida has no Zombie Gnomes!*

I'm currently at a bus station in North Carolina on my way to present this vital information to the American President.

Curses! I hear the rustling of Zombie Gnomes in the underbrush. If only the bus driver hadn't stopped me from bringing my ultimate weapon on board! I wasn't expecting to encounter a Gnome infestation on my trip, and I am unarmed save for a few emergency paper clips and a pretzel stick passed down from my great-great-grandfather.

I cannot spare another moment. I must record the secret to destroying Zombie Gnomes at once, in these very pages. Then I will continue onward to Washington, D.C., to consult with the President. If the President should happen to be unavailable, I shall consult with the Vice President. If the Vice President is unavailable, then the Speaker of the House. If the Speaker is unavailable, the President Pro Tempore of the Senate. At some point I may break for lunch. I believe I shall have the liver and onions. If not that, the French dip. If not that, perhaps I shall inquire as to the soup of the day. Then, refreshed, I shall return to intense discussion with the President Pro Tempore, unless he or she happens to be unavailable, in which case I shall speak to the Secretary of State. If the Secretary of State is unavailable, then the Secretary of the Treasury. If the Secretary of the Treasury is unavailable, then ARRRGH THEY'RE UPON ME MY LEGS MY LEGS AHHHHHHHH thud.

Van Poort's book ends abruptly. It looks like he was about to reveal a vital weapon against Zombie Gnomes when, probably inevitably, the Gnomes got him. The most frustrating part is that he could have written the information down, but for some reason he decided to transcribe his screams instead. That was weird.

So what is the anti-Gnome weapon Van Poort discovered? Why are there no Gnomes in Florida? I have no choice. I have to resume Dr. Griebel's research, with the goal of finding a way to stop the Zombie Gnomes.

I've already started making sketches. This is hard.

. . . .

I need more Zombie Gnomes for my experiments. Dr. Griebel took her test Gnomes with her, packed into poster tubes for easy access (the list of really bad ideas on Dr. Griebel's part keeps growing the more I think about it), and by now even creatures as stupid as Zombie Gnomes have learned not to come into the lab garden.

I'll set up some traps. I need more Gnomes! More Gnomes, I say!

•• • • • ••

Success! I heard something fall into the snake pit I dug in the front lawn. From the sound of it, I got a whole hjorde of Zombie Gnomes. Wow, they've really kicking up a fuss. I'll go collect them and put them into cages.

Update:
Never mind. It's my mom. She came to remind me about my dad's birthday party. I'd better pick up some Neosporin and a necktie.

• ••• • •••

Well, here I am at my dad's sixtieth birthday party. Aunt Rose baked a cake, Aunt Mary made her famous fried chicken, and my cousin's flower shop filled the front lawn with balloons and sixty of those pink plastic lawn flamingoes.

I guess I got a little obsessed back at the lab, but I can't stop thinking about Van Poort's journal. Just what did he discover in Florida that could repel Zombie Gnomes? Orange juice? Palm trees? Those six-toed cats that live at Hemingway's house? I spent a week reading up on Ponce de Leon and his quest for the Fountain of Youth, but I'm no closer to figuring this out today than I was when I first learned of the Zombie Gnomes.

I'll try to get a good night's sleep in my old bed, at any rate.

Maybe a fresh perspective will put me back in the pink.

Update:

So much for sleeping in. I woke up at dawn to the all-too-familiar sounds of Zombie Gnomes rampaging and feeding. Did they follow me? Did I literally bring my work along with me? Whatever the case, it looks like South Main Street is going to have a hard time putting together an ultimate Frisbee team for this year's block party.

They just took down Mr. Johnson from next door. Now I'm not sure if we'll have enough hands left for a late-night game of euchre.

And there go the Hendersons.

But for some reason the Zombie Gnomes aren't attacking our house. Do they know I'm here? Do they have something sinister planned for me?

No, that can't be right. They've never displayed the cognitive capacity to consistently recognize individual humans. My parents don't have pets, so it can't be that . . . and they're chasing after the Whitmores' wiener dog right now, anyway. But they've definitely avoiding our house. They won't even set foot on our lawn.

Which is too bad, since it would be funny to get a photo of them playing around with all those balloons and the sixty pink—

Eureka!

. ...

My experiments have all but confirmed it. I know what Zombie Gnomes fear! Now I just need to contact an authority who will listen to me.

.. . .

GILLY'S GREEN THUMB GAB

Ruthless Retribution and Miniature Massacres

Dear Gilly,
The western perimeter has been breached. Please send machetes and a riding mower.

Your loyal minion,
Dave

Dear Dave,
We've been out of fuel for the riding mowers since Zombie Gnomes destroyed our route to the Gas N Gulp. It's time to rediscover an ecologically responsible alternative to the push mower. As described in my column "Green Growing and Fit Farming," as a bonus, it's great exercise!

She Whose Wrath Is as the Frost
Upon the Bean Sprouts,
Gilly

Dear Gilly,
Push mowers are the worst and you know it. Those little beards get stuck in the blades.

Still minning, or whatever minions do,
Dave

Dear Gilly,

My name is Barbara Wong, and at some point I was studying for my PhD in horticulture. I'm writing to you because no other news outlet will believe my story. After months of studying Zombie Gnomes, I've discovered their natural predator.

Flamingoes.

The late lost missing-in-action Zombie Gnome hunter Ranier Van Poort discovered that Zombie Gnomes had infested every state in the United States except Florida. That was my first clue.

When Zombie Gnomes invaded my parents' neighborhood in Ohio, every family on my block—except mine—was devoured by the tiny invaders. The miniature invasion came to a complete halt when the Zombie Gnomes encountered the plastic flamingoes on our front lawn, and for the first time in my long, long months of observing them, the little monsters knew FEAR.

And why not? The flamingo is the Zombie Gnome's only natural predator. The flamingoes' long, thin legs are too tough for Gnome teeth to penetrate. The sharp, scooped bill of the flamingo can behead and devour a Zombie Gnome in one fell swoop. The dazzling pink plumage of the flamingo sears the very retinas of the Zombie Gnomes, whose forest habitat consists of dull and muted colors.

Or maybe the flamingoes make them think back fondly on their favorite episodes of *Miami Vice*.

So take this advice and share it with all your readers, far and wide! Take shelter at your local zoo! Don't wait until spring break to visit Florida! Cover your yard with as many plastic lawn flamingoes as possible! Wear pink at all times, just to be safe (and because you can never wear too much pink)!

I can only hope I've relayed this message in time. And that there are no continents entirely bereft of flamingoes where the Zombie Gnomes can flourish yet again. But what are the odds of that?

Sincerely,
Barbara Wong (don't call me "Babs")

P.S. Dave, is that you? You left a sandwich in the lab fridge, but you didn't label it and we weren't sure if we should throw it out or not.

Dear Dave,

Find this "Barbara Wong" and bring her to me. We shall parlay.

**She Whose Name the Foot-High
Dead Dare Not Speak**

EDITOR'S NOTE: Zombie Gnome historians (both of them) agree that the most significant Zombie Gnome event on U.S. soil occurred at the 100th annual Monroeville Winter Flowerganza in beautiful Monroeville, Pennsylvania. Although mainstream news coverage of this event was sparse, apart from a coupon in the Monroeville Gazette, I was able to piece together a real-time look at the incident through the Monroeville Garden Society's InstaGarden social media account. Be advised that this report is not for the faint of heart.

MONROEVILLE GARDEN SOCIETY MONGARDEN 3H
♥ Gardengeek, HortoCulture, and 82 others liked

Welcome to the 100th annual Monroeville Winter Flowerganza, the biggest garden convention of the year!

MONROEVILLE GARDEN SOCIETY MONGARDEN 3H
♥ Mums the Word, GreenMenace, and 78 others liked

Several attendees reporting bites from small animals or people (???). Please take complaints to Guest Services.

MONROEVILLE GARDEN SOCIETY MONGARDEN 2H
♥ Flower Child, Gardengeek, and 77 others liked

The Monroeville Garden Society does not condone the unhinged rants of the woman standing on the Butterfly Gazebo.

MONROEVILLE GARDEN SOCIETY MONGARDEN 1H 41M
♥ Two Lips, Rose McGrowin', and 77 others liked

Everyone please move away from the Butterfly Gazebo. That is not an approved event and now she has some kind of hand cannon.

MONROEVILLE GARDEN SOCIETY MONGARDEN 15M
♥ **Spore Loser, NastyTurtium, and 48 others liked**

Oh crud, she's firing.

MONROEVILLE GARDEN SOCIETY MONGARDEN 14M
♥ **HortoCulture, Flower Bedlam, and 48 others liked**

What are those things?

MONROEVILLE GARDEN SOCIETY MONGARDEN 1H 20M
♥ **PushLittleDaisies, This Bud's for You, and 67 others liked**

Dr. Griebel now waving cannon, screaming something about "When there is no more room in the potting shed, the dead will walk the earth."

MONROEVILLE GARDEN SOCIETY MONGARDEN 1H 19M
♥ **Carrothead, Beetmaniac, and 63 others liked**

The Monroeville Garden Society apologizes to our visitors who just wanted to attend the Year-Round Veggies panel in peace.

MONROEVILLE GARDEN SOCIETY MONGARDEN 1H 8M
♥ **DimBulb, Gardengeek, and 60 others liked**

What's in that hand cannon, anyway? Can anyone get a close-up?

MONROEVILLE GARDEN SOCIETY MONGARDEN 1H
♥ **Mr. Compost, Sneaky Peat, and 59 others liked**

Thanks to Sneaky Peat for the photo!

MONROEVILLE GARDEN SOCIETY MONGARDEN 45M
♥ **Pruning Machine, Lawn Dart, and 56 others liked**

Dr. Griebel's threats of revenge will not be tolerated. We
have good reason to dismiss her from the landscaping
Q&A.

MONROEVILLE GARDEN SOCIETY MONGARDEN 44M
♥ **Lawn Dart, Mums the Word, and 53 others liked**

As she well knows, the Winter Flowerganza does not
permit tacky lawn ornaments.

MONROEVILLE GARDEN SOCIETY MONGARDEN 33M
♥ **Gardengeek, Bean There, and 50 others liked**

EVERYONE GET AWAY FROM THE GAZEBO. Dr. Griebel is aiming the hand cannon.

MONROEVILLE GARDEN SOCIETY MONGARDEN 30M
♥ **Gardengeek, Rose McGrowin', and 50 others liked**

I know we all kind of want to see what it does, but have some sense, people.

MONROEVILLE GARDEN SOCIETY MONGARDEN 23M
♥ **Gardengeek, Jaunty Rake, and 50 others liked**

Gardengeek, you've liked every single one of these posts and I can tell from your comments that YOU'RE STILL AT THE DANG GAZEBO.

MONROEVILLE GARDEN SOCIETY MONGARDEN 15M

♥ Spore Loser, NastyTurtium, and 48 others liked

Oh crud, she's firing.

MONROEVILLE GARDEN SOCIETY MONGARDEN 14M

♥ HortoCulture, Flower Bedlam, and 48 others liked

What are those things?

MONROEVILLE GARDEN SOCIETY MONGARDEN 12M
♥ **Flower Bedlam, DimBulb, and 40 others liked**

Dr. Griebel: "Fly, my pretties! Aim for their heads!"

MONROEVILLE GARDEN SOCIETY MONGARDEN 10M
♥ **Cultivar Warrior, Gardengeek, and 30 others liked**

oh no they're everywhere!

MONROEVILLE GARDEN SOCIETY MONGARDEN 9M
♥ **LustyTomato, Two Lips, and 20 others liked**

this is the stupidest way to die

MONROEVILLE GARDEN SOCIETY MONGARDEN 7M

♥ Tower of Flower, TooMuchZucchiniBread, and 10 others liked

MONROEVILLE GARDEN SOCIETY MONGARDEN 3M

♥ **Gardengeek liked**

MONROEVILLE GARDEN SOCIETY MONGARDEN 2M

NOM NOM NOM

MONROEVILLE GARDEN SOCIETY MONGARDEN 1M

Sorry for the spotty updates, journal. I've been recruited into the Glorious Green Thumb Army, which sounds impressive but turns out to be a gardening columnist/blogger named Gilly and her wild-eyed fans. They rescued Dave from the Zombie Gnomes and now he's the G.G.T. Army's most enthusiastic member. He made himself a uniform and everything. I guess it's nice to see him cultivating a hobby and, you know, alive.

I have to hand it to Gilly's cult anti-Gnome army: It's efficient. I shared my findings about the offensive properties of flamingos, and within hours they were rounding up plastic lawn flamingos by the thousands, not to mention dozens of real live birds. They're a little cagey about where all these flamingos are coming from. Gilly tells me not to look a gift horse in the mouth, and also that someone named Tony is shipping several boxcars full of live flamingos from Argentina and don't ask any questions.

My biggest concern is that we haven't had the chance to test the flamingos against a real Zombie Gnome attack. If my hypothesis is wrong, I'll have piles of pink birds and a mob of disappointed unhinged cultists freedom fighters to deal with.

Update:
Social media is blowing up ("Blowing up"? Is that something people still say? I've been in grad school for six years and I have no idea how normal people talk) with news of a Zombie Gnome invasion led by my own mentor, Dr. Griebel. There are photos confirming the whole story. I wish I could say I was surprised.

Gilly says it's time for the Glorious Army to meet the enemy head-on. I'll be carpooling with a former orchid thief, two organic gardeners with VEGAN LIFE tattoos, a trunkful of lawn flamingos, and Dave.

Update:
Dave has been barred from the passenger seat because he only wants to play the Black-Eyed Peas.

***

I hardly know where to begin to paint for you a word picture of the strange scene before my eyes, like something out of a Rankin-Bass special about the Book of Revelations. Gnomes are everywhere. They push cunning little wheelbarrows loaded with ammo, and a bunch of them are building a charming Bavarian-style throne of skulls. You can barely tell this wasteland was once a home and garden show. Dave says it might be an improvement. The war has given him a cynical sense of humor.

There are still a few people from the garden show hiding in the debris. I asked a man what he saw. "I saw a kinda red-and-green streak and then zingo! Something smacked into the ground," he said. "Danged if it wasn't a little beardy man flying out of the gol-darn sky."

I asked him to please stop talking like an old-timey hick. "Sorry," he said. "Reckon it's the shock."

I wish I could convey the atmosphere, the background of this phantasmagorical scene. Police are trying to rope off the roadway leading to the convention center, but it's no use. The Zombie Gnomes are swarming everywhere. Wherever Dr. Griebel is, I have to admit she was right. They can be trained.

I told Gilly this. She said, "We've trained, too." She cocked a lawn flamingo. "Let's do some landscaping."

Update:
Can't write now. Battle has been joined.

It wasn't an easy victory. But once we unleashed the flamingos, the battle was decided. I'm not sure which were more deadly to the Zombie Gnomes: the real flamingos, which seemed to instantly recognize the Gnomes as their rightful prey, or the plastic flamingos, which are amazingly good for whacking those gross little buggers around.

With Gnomes flying left and right, Dr. Griebel climbed onto the throne of skulls and tried to bark commands. "Attack! Attack, I say! My wee zombie army will not be defeated! I am invincible! Invincible, I s—"

And then the Zombie Gnomes ate her.

Turns out they weren't that trainable after all.

The Glorious Green Thumb Army is trying to explain everything to the authorities now. It's not going too well. Gilly thinks we should receive the Medal of Honor and the city should be renamed "Gillyburg." The mayor is trying to compromise with an offer of two gift certificates to the Red Lobster and a free car wash.

I'm going to go sleep in Dave's car.

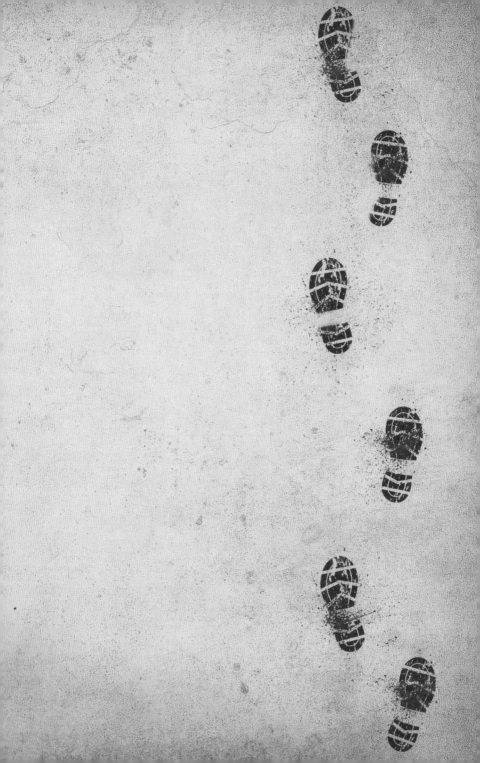

GILLY'S GREEN THUMB GAB

Fame, Fortune, and Forsythia

Dear Gilly,

Congratulations on your new TV reality show, *Gnome Man's Land*! I can't wait to see you transform ordinary homeowners' properties into Gnome-destroying fortresses. A little disappointed that you stepped down as God-Empress of the Glorious Green Thumb Army. Is it okay to continue to worship you?

Chloe

Dear Chloe,

Worship away, as long as you tune in to the show! Despite the title (the network insisted!), I'll be covering so much more than Zombie Gnomes. With Gnomes all but eradicated, I can expand my focus to taking on elves, leprechauns, Little Men, and overaggressive flamingos. Especially the flamingos. They've been getting out of hand lately.

Gilly

Dear Gilly,

Just a tip for Mo, who wrote in last month to ask about the flammability of Zombie Gnomes. It just so happens I've been running experiments to answer exactly that question. Short answer: Zombie Gnomes are either flammable or inflammable, whichever one means more fire. On a recent research expedition I discovered a previously unknown subspecies of Gnome that lives in Irish peat bogs. Peat Zombie Gnomes go up like a signal flare and burn for hours. We may be able to use them to eradicate ordinary hjordes from hard-to-reach places: Just set a Peat Gnome on fire and send it down the hole. Or, you know, wherever you've got Zombie Gnomes.

Tell Mo good luck and happy hunting!

Barbara

Dear Barbara,

From Barbara's pen to your eyes, readers! We're always lucky to get a new tip from the world's foremost Zombie Gnome biologist. Glad to hear grad school is going well, Barb!

Gilly

Dear Gilly,

I was at my local garden center with a couple of friends, picking up tomato plants, when a wild-eyed stranger in tattered lederhosen stopped me. He told me a long, terrible tale of battling Zombie Gnomes around the world. There were also several lengthy digressions about the pretzel industry and why I shouldn't eat hamburgers. He claimed to have narrowly survived a Gnome attack by bludgeoning an entire rampaging hjorde with the unfinished manuscript of his memoirs.

"If there resides in you any milk of human kindness," he rasped, "tell the so-called experts on the Red-Hatted Menace that Ranier Van Poort lives and there is much you do not yet know. Speak to me if you want to live!"

Any advice?

Elena

Dear Elena,
Do I have advice? *Do I have advice?* Good lord, this is the most serious matter ever brought to my attention. You absolutely must wait until at *least* early summer to plant tomatoes! Don't think I don't know how temptingly those young heirloom varieties beckon, but be strong! Unless you're growing from seeds in a greenhouse or a sunny window box, focus on spring veggies and save the tomatoes and peppers for hot weather. I've said this again and again, but somehow it never gets through. Hmph.

Gilly

Dear Gilly,
Thanks to the quick work of the Glorious Green Thumb Army, Zombie Gnomes seem to have been driven back. It's been days since I saw even one report of a pointy-hat sighting, and weeks since any real attacks. But are the Zombie Gnomes really gone? How can we be sure we've wiped them out?

Jason

Dear Jason,
As I always say, constant vigilance is the price of not getting your knees chewed off. That said, our glorious uprising rained destruction upon the Zombie Gnomes and salted the earth where they had stood. (Metaphorically, of course! I do not condone salting good soil!) I believe it's safe to say that we've heard the last high-pitched groan from the once-mighty, now vanquished, Zombie Gnome menace.

Gilly

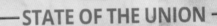

—— STATE OF THE UNION ——

"EVERYTHING FINE AND DANDY"

WASHINGTON, D.C.—

After a tumultuous three-week period during which nearly 20,000 Americans were reported "missing, eaten, or both," the Centers for Disease Control issued a statement reassuring the public that "everything is fine and dandy," that there was "no zombie outbreak," and "just please stay calm, remain indoors, and don't eat anyone just please don't eat anyone."

Newly elected Senator I. M. Threegnomesinasuit from Wisconsin announced his full support of the CDC's report, although he was quoted as saying, "Please put barbecue sauce on feets and stomp around in high grass every morning" during a bizarre, rambling interview on Capitol Hill this afternoon. "Ketchup okay, too."

When asked to clarify his statements, the senator looked to the sky, shrieked loudly, then scampered off into the woods, proclaiming, "Me human like you! Me totally not three gnomes in a suit!"

The President could not be reached for comment, as he was already en route to Scandinavia for a summit with the Emperor of Finland, King Reilly Reilly GnöttaGnöme of Helsinki.

SHAENON K. GARRITY is a cartoonist and science fiction writer best known for the webcomics *Narbonic* and *Skin Horse.*

ANDREW FARAGO is the curator of the Cartoon Art Museum in San Francisco and author of the Harvey Award-winning *Teenage Mutant Ninja Turtles: The Ultimate Visual History.* Shaenon and Andrew live in Berkeley, California.

BRYAN HEEMSKERK is a mega concept artist and illustrator and a mega dad with three kids from Toronto, Ontario. He is known for his work on video games such as Halcyon 6.